The Easy Art of Appliqué

Techniques for Hand, Machine, and Fusible Appliqué

Mimi Dietrich &
Roxi Eppler

That Patchwork Place®

Credits

Editor-in-Chief .... Barbara Weiland
Technical Editor .... Kerry I. Hoffman
Managing Editor .... Greg Sharp
Copy Editor .... Liz McGehee
Proofreaders .... Leslie Phillips
                                  Kathleen Timko
Text and Cover Designer .... Cheryl Senecal
Photographer .... Brent Kane
Illustrators .... Laurel Strand
                                  Brian Metz
Illustration Assistant .... Lisa McKenney

The Easy Art of Appliqué
© 1994 by Mimi Dietrich and Roxi Eppler
That Patchwork Place, Inc., PO Box 118, Bothell, WA 98041-0118 USA

Printed in the United States of America
99 98 97 96 95   6 5 4 3 2

Dedication: To our appliqué students

Library of Congress Cataloging-in-Publication Data

Dietrich, Mimi.
   The easy art of appliqué / Mimi Dietrich and Roxi Eppler.
      p.   cm. — (The joy of quilting)
   ISBN 1-56477-081-8 :
   1. Appliqué—Patterns. 2. Machine appliqué. 3. Quilts.
I. Eppler, Roxi, II. Title. III. Series.
TT779.D543   1994
746.44'5—dc20   94-31139
                                    CIP

Table of Contents

Introduction

Many beginning quilters admire appliquéd quilts and think that the designs are far too intricate and intimidating for their skill level. This is simply not true. With some practice, all designs are easy to accomplish.

The definition of the word appliqué is "to apply." Instead of sewing fabric pieces together to make patchwork designs, appliqué designs are cut from selected fabrics and sewn on top of a background fabric to create beautiful designs.

Appliqué makes it easy to create intricate designs with curves, flowers, and realistic shapes. Traditional appliqué is done by hand, but machine appliqué has gained popularity in recent years. The most wonderful thing about appliqué is that there are so many different ways to do it!

The Easy Art of Appliqué includes Mimi's directions for hand appliqué techniques, followed by Roxi's directions for machine appliqué. In addition, they have included directions for fusible appliqué as an alternative quick-and-easy appliqué method.

Join these two enthusiastic red-heads as Mimi and Roxi demonstrate their favorite methods for appliqué! They have designed quilts for this book so that you can share the easy art of appliqué.

If you have never appliquéd, begin with the traditional hand and machine techniques. You can practice preparing and stitching hand or machine appliqué pieces by making the simple heart- and star-shaped appliqué project that appears on page 43. This project is great for mastering the basic techniques—appliquéing pieces with straight edges, curves, and inside and outside points.

Next, stitch Mimi's "Welcome to Baltimore." "Miniature Violets" adds dimensional appliqué techniques to a wonderful miniature quilt.

If you prefer machine appliqué, practice on Roxi's "Cockscomb" quilt on page 50, or create a garden of flowers with "Folk Flowers."

For added fun, use fusible appliqué techniques to create "A Year of Friendship"—twelve little designs combined into a calendar wall hanging. With this one, you may choose to repeat one design for a delightfully special quilt. (See the "Button Baskets" quilt photo on page 31.)

All of the quilts in this book can be stitched with hand or machine techniques. Enjoy these designs and have fun learning the easy art of appliqué!

Hand Appliqué

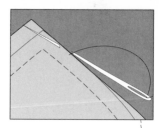

Selecting Fabrics for Appliqué

Keep in mind when you select fabrics that you need fabric for two purposes: the background fabric and the appliqué pieces.

Appliqué background fabrics are usually solid light colors or small prints and stripes that complement the appliqué design. A bold print, plaid, or stripe may make it difficult to see the appliquéd design.

White background fabrics add brightness and clarity to pastel appliqués. Off-white backgrounds enhance the richness of darker appliqué palettes. White-on-white or white-on-muslin prints make lovely backgrounds for stitchers who like a subtle print rather than a solid. A fabulous "tea-dyed" print gives an antique glow to quilts. Appliqués stitched on a dark background create a dramatic effect.

Choose fabrics for the appliqué pieces that are appropriate for the design. Consider the color and print size for the pattern you are stitching.

Preview the fabrics you choose by making a window template. Simply cut the shape of your appliqué piece as a "window" in a piece of paper. Place the window over the fabric to view the effect.

To determine a color palette for your quilt, it's fun to first choose a multicolored fabric that you love. Use the colors contained in this "inspiration" fabric as the color scheme for your quilt. The inspiration fabric may also be used for appliqué pieces, borders to frame your design, or on the back of the quilt.

Solid fabrics are always "safe" to use, but printed fabrics may make your designs more exciting. Fabric printed in different values of one color can be very effective in representing features found in flowers and leaves. Tone-on-tone fabrics, such as dark green printed over a slightly lighter green, look like a solid but with a subtle texture. In addition, the designs of printed fabrics create lines that may be used to emphasize veins in leaves or textures in flower petals.

Fabrics printed with flowers and leaves are wonderful to use in appliqué. Cut out whole flowers or individual petals and leaves to give a realistic look to your appliqués. Use basket-weave prints for baskets or wood-grain prints for stems.

By using several values of the same color, you can add realism to appliquéd flowers. Fabrics printed by the same manufacturer are often available in different prints with coordinating colors. Hand-dyed fabrics in light-to-dark gradations are wonderful for shading flowers and leaves to achieve a three-dimensional look.

Tie-dyed fabrics are exciting to use because the light and dark areas of the fabric blend together well. A leaf can be cut so that two tones are positioned on either side of the center to create a vein. If you use a shaded fabric for flower petals, position the darker area of the fabric in the center of the flower.

Be brave and try using the right and wrong sides of the same fabric to shade flowers, ribbons, and bows. It may seem unusual to use the wrong side, but wonderful effects often result.

Large-scale prints may seem inappropriate for appliqué, but a small piece cut from a specific area may make the perfect flower petal or bird wing. Use your window template to help you decide.

Make a color "paste-up" of your colors before you start to stitch if you have enough fabric. Trace your pattern onto a sheet of paper, cut the appliqué shapes out of your fabric shapes, then glue them to the design. This helps you make decisions about the color arrangements before you begin stitching. Use this as a placement guide as you stitch.

Fabrics with 100% cotton fiber content are easier to appliqué than synthetic fabrics, which tend to fray more than cotton and are often slippery. Sometimes, however, the "perfect" fabric contains synthetic fibers, and it's worth a little extra care to use a special fabric in your design. Contemporary appliqué artists often use a variety of fabrics, including lamé and satin, but these are not recommended for beginners.

Prewash all fabrics to preshrink and to test for colorfastness. Wash dark and light colors separately. Sometimes it is necessary to wash and rinse dark-colored fabrics several times to get rid of excess dye. To test a fabric for colorfastness, cut a small piece, wet it, and place it on a scrap of background fabric. If color shows up on the background scrap, wash the fabric again or choose a different fabric. Take the time to make sure your fabrics are preshrunk and colorfast. This ensures that your finished quilt will not shrink and that the colors won't bleed onto each other when the quilt is laundered.

Press fabrics to remove wrinkles so that the appliqué pieces and backgrounds can be cut accurately. Some quilters apply spray starch or sizing to help give fabrics extra body, making them easier to handle.

Supplies and Tools

There are many products available in quilt and fabric shops that will help you successfully complete your appliqué projects.

Needles

The most important consideration when choosing a needle is the size. A sharp, fine needle glides easily through the edges of appliqué pieces, so your stitches are small and inconspicuous. The higher the number, the finer the needle. Try a size 10 or 12 for the best stitching results.

The type of needle used for hand appliqué depends on personal choice. Some appliqué stitchers use short quilting needles (Betweens) because they feel closer to the stitching. Some quilters find longer needles (Sharps) easier to control. Long needles with large eyes (crewels) may be easier to thread. An even longer type of needle (milliner's or straw) works well as a tool

for "needle-turning" the appliqué edge as you stitch it to the background.

Quilting needle
(Between) ━━━━━━━━━━━━━
Sharp ━━━━━━━━━━
Crewel ◯━━━━━━━━
Milliner's ━━━━━━━━━━━━━━

Try different needles to find the one most comfortable for you. If a fine needle is difficult to thread, use a needle threader to insert the thread through the eye of the needle.

Thread

Thread used for appliqué should match the color of the appliqué pieces rather than the background fabric. Many shades of thread are required for designs with many different-colored pieces. If it is not possible to match the color exactly, choose thread that is a little darker than the fabric. For appliqué fabrics that contain many colors, choose a thread that blends with the predominant color.

All-cotton thread works well for hand stitching appliqués. It is pliable and blends invisibly into the edges of the appliqués. If cotton thread is not available in just the right color, use cotton-covered polyester thread. Sometimes it's necessary to use thread that you have available in your sewing area at that moment. If so, make sure the thread is strong and closely matches the color of your appliqué pieces.

Embroidery floss can be used to match colors on small appliqué pieces. It should not be used on large pieces, however, because the thread tends to fray and become thin after it has been drawn through the fabric numerous times.

White or light-colored thread should always be used for basting. Dye from dark thread can leave small dots of color on light fabrics.

Pins

Use small straight pins to pin-baste appliqué pieces to the background fabric. Small, ½"- or ¾"-long sequin pins are wonderful because they do not get in the way of the thread as you stitch.

Scissors

A small pair of scissors with sharp blades is essential for clipping threads, clipping inside points, and trimming appliqué pieces.

Glue Stick

A water-soluble glue stick is handy for "basting" pieces in position instead of basting by hand.

Fabric Markers

Fabric markers are used to trace appliqué designs onto the background fabric and to mark each appliqué piece. Use silver marking pencils, water-erasable pens, or fine-lead mechanical pencils for light fabrics. For dark fabrics, use sharp chalk pencils in light colors or a silver marking pencil. It is always wise to test markers on a scrap of fabric to make sure they can be removed.

Template Plastic and Permanent Markers

Use template plastic to make patterns for the appliqué designs. You can make templates by gluing paper pattern pieces to cardboard, but plastic templates are more durable and accurate. Trace the designs onto the plastic using a fine-tip permanent marking pen.

Freezer Paper

Available at most grocery stores, white freezer paper has a shiny plastic coating on one side and an uncoated side. The coated side softens and adheres to fabric when you apply a dry, warm iron to the uncoated side. Use it to prepare appliqués that require smoothly turned edges.

Tweezers

A pair of small tweezers makes it easy to remove freezer paper after you have appliquéd a piece to the background.

Pillow

Place a 12"–14" pillow in your lap as you hand appliqué. It provides a nice pincushion, a comfortable place to rest your hands, and helps improve your posture as you work.

Sewing Machine

Machine appliqué requires a zigzag sewing machine that is in good working order. Start with a sharp, new, size 75/11 or 70/10 needle in your machine.

Getting Ready to Appliqué

Use the following key for distinguishing the right and the wrong sides of fabric and freezer paper.

Right side of fabric   Wrong side of fabric   Uncoated side of freezer paper   Shiny (coated) side of freezer paper

To prepare for hand appliqué, you must mark the design onto the background fabric, make templates for each appliqué shape, and then trace the shapes onto the selected appliqué fabrics and cut them out.

Marking the Background Fabric

The background fabric for appliqué is usually cut in a rectangle or square, or in long strips for borders. If the finished size of an appliqué block is 10" square, cut the block 10½" x 10½" to allow for seams. It is even better to cut the square an inch larger to compensate for the fabric "drawing up" during appliqué, then trim it to the correct size after completing the appliqué. Cut accurate background squares using your rotary cutter, mat, and a large, square acrylic ruler.

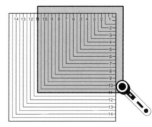

To place the appliqué pieces onto the background fabric accurately, mark the design onto the fabric. It is easy to trace the design onto light background fabrics.

1. Place the fabric right side up over the pattern so that the design is in the correct position on the background piece.

2. Trace the design carefully. If you use a silver marking pencil or a water-erasable pen, trace the marks exactly. Remember to test these markers first on a scrap of fabric to make sure you can remove them with cold water. If you use a mechanical pencil, trace slightly inside the pattern lines. The lines will be covered by the appliquéd pieces after they are stitched on, so you don't have to worry about removing the lines.

Some quilters use a method of minimal marking for their appliqués. For example, a single dot denotes placement for a circle; two dots show placement for the ends of leaves.

For dark background fabrics, a little more effort is involved.

1. Trace the design carefully with a white or yellow chalk pencil.

2. Using a light box or table is helpful when you trace the design onto dark fabrics. If you do not have a light box, tape the pattern to a window or storm door on a sunny day. Then center your fabric over the pattern, tape the fabric to the glass, and trace the design. You can also create your own light box by opening your dining room table and placing a storm window over the table-leaf opening. Place a lamp or flashlight on the floor to shine through the glass like a light box. Place your pattern on the glass, then your fabric on top of the pattern. The light will shine through so that you can easily trace your design.

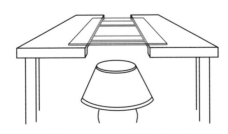

Make your own "light box."

Pattern Overlay

If it is too difficult for you to trace the design onto your background fabric or if you do not wish to mark directly on your background fabric, try the following technique. Quilters prefer to use this method when a pattern has many layers of appliqué pieces.

1. Make a pattern overlay by tracing the design onto a piece of clear template plastic (or use acetate or tracing paper) that is the same size as your background piece. Trace the design onto the plastic using a permanent marker.

2. Place the plastic over the background fabric. To position each appliqué piece, lift up the plastic, slide each piece under the appropriate marking, then pin or baste the appliqué to the background fabric.

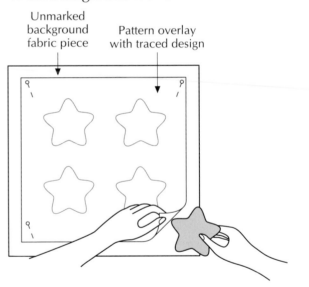

Unmarked background fabric piece

Pattern overlay with traced design

Making Appliqué Templates

Appliqué patterns do not always provide separate "pattern pieces" for appliqué. Trace the elements of each appliqué design to create the pattern templates you need.

Making Plastic Templates

Make templates for the appliqué pieces by tracing the appliqué-design pieces onto template plastic. Templates may also be made by using paper patterns glued to cardboard, but plastic templates are more durable and accurate.

1. Place the plastic over the pattern and trace each design with a fine-line permanent marker. *Do not add seam allowances.*

2. Cut out templates on the traced lines so they are the exact size of the design pieces.

If a design is repeated in a quilt, you only need one plastic template for each design. For example, you need one heart template to make the four hearts in the "Wish Upon a Star" quilt on page 43.

Making Freezer-Paper Templates

Make freezer-paper templates for appliqué by tracing the designs directly onto freezer paper.

1. Place the freezer paper, coated side down, over the design and trace the design onto the *uncoated side* with a fine-lead pencil.

Uncoated side of freezer paper

2. Cut out the templates on the traced lines so that they are the exact size of the design pieces.

Symmetrical designs are traced directly from the pattern to the paper. For asymmetrical designs, like the sunflowers in the "Folk Flowers" quilt on page 34, you must trace a reverse (mirror) image of the pattern piece. To trace a reverse image, turn the pattern over and place it on a light box or against a bright window. Or, accurately trace the design onto tracing paper, then turn the tracing paper over, lay your freezer paper on top (shiny side down), and trace the design.

For designs that are repeated, make a plastic template and trace around it onto the freezer paper. This ensures that your freezer-paper pieces are all the same size.

Cut multiple layers of freezer paper for repeated pieces by stapling up to four layers of freezer paper together. Trace the design on the top layer, placing the staples in the space that will be cut away. The staples hold your paper together as you cut accurate templates.

If you need a sturdier freezer-paper template, iron two layers of freezer paper together.

Cutting Appliqués

Appliqué designs do not usually provide grain lines to aid in positioning the templates on the fabric. If possible, place the templates on the appliqué fabric so that the grain runs in the same direction as the background fabric.

Designs that have "inside points" (such as hearts) or curves (such as leaves) can be placed on the bias grain of the fabric. The bias prevents fraying at inside points and makes it easier to ease fabric around curves.

In many appliqué designs, you may want the cut piece to include a special design printed on the fabric. In this case, disregard grain lines and enjoy the way that the fabric and the appliqué design work together.

To aid in selecting specific areas of fabrics when you want to get just the right effect, cut the shape of your appliqué piece in a piece of paper to make a "window." Move the window over your fabric to locate the right area.

Take your time planning your appliqué pieces and you will be pleased with the results.

Using Appliqué Templates

Plastic Templates

1. Place the template right side up on the right side of the fabric. A sheet of fine sandpaper placed under your fabric will prevent the fabric from slipping as you work. A small piece of double-sided tape on the back of the template will also keep it secure.

2. Trace around the template, marking on the right side of the fabric. Use a mechanical pencil for light fabrics or a sharp chalk pencil for dark fabrics. Water-erasable markers can be used, but often the line is not fine enough to be accurate. When trac-

ing several pieces onto your fabric, leave at least ½" separation between each piece.

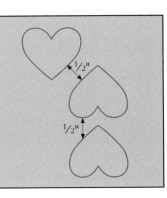

Right side
of fabric

3. Cut out each fabric piece, adding ¼"-wide seam allowances on all sides. The seam allowance will be turned under to create the finished edge of the appliqué.

Freezer-Paper Templates

Freezer-paper templates may be used either on top or on the back of the appliqué fabric.

Freezer Paper on the Back

1. Place the freezer-paper template with the shiny side facing the *wrong side* of the appliqué fabric.

2. Press the freezer paper to the fabric, using a hot, dry iron (no steam or spray). Let the piece cool.

3. Cut out the fabric appliqué piece, adding a ¼"-wide seam allowance of fabric around the outside edge of the freezer paper.

4. For this method, asymmetrical shapes must be traced in reverse.

Freezer Paper on Top

1. Place the freezer-paper template with the *shiny* side facing the *right side* of the appliqué fabric. Press the freezer paper to the fabric, using a hot, dry iron (no steam or spray). Let the piece cool.

2. Cut out the fabric appliqué piece, adding a ¼"-wide seam allowance around the outside edge of the freezer paper.

3. For this method, trace all shapes onto freezer paper as they appear on the design. Do not trace asymmetrical designs in reverse.

Preparing Appliqués

There are many different techniques for preparing appliqué pieces. Some methods work better than others in different situations and with different fabrics.

Eight different methods for appliqué preparation follow. Each one uses a heart shape for illustration. Experiment and try each method to determine your favorite. Choose your preferred technique and enjoy it with the knowledge that you can always substitute another when it will provide better results.

Preparation Basics

Before appliquéing the pieces to the background, prepare the appliqué pieces by turning under the seam allowances carefully. Edges should be smooth and evenly turned. Care in this step will help you place the appliqués accurately on the background fabric.

Turn under the seam allowances, rolling any traced lines to the back, and baste around each piece with light-colored thread. Traced lines should not show on the front or along the edge of the appliqué. See "Basting Practice" on facing page.

Try looking at the right side of the piece while you turn under the edge and baste near the fold. This helps to keep the piece neat and accurate as you concentrate on the smooth shape of the piece. If you keep your stitches near the fold, you will be sure to catch the seam allowance.

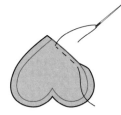

If one appliqué piece overlaps another, it is unnecessary to turn under edges that will be covered by other appliqué pieces. These edges should lie flat under the covering appliqué piece.

Basting Practice

Practice basting the edges of a heart-shaped appliqué and a swag. Make a freezer-paper template, using the template below to cut a heart from fabric scraps. With this simple shape, you can practice straight edges, curves, an outside point, and an inside point. To practice with inside curves, make a sample freezer-paper template of the swag as shown on page 12. You will be basting through the appliqué fabric and the freezer-paper template. Press the freezer-paper templates to the *wrong side* of the appliqué fabric, using a hot, dry iron. Cut out the fabric appliqué piece, adding a ¼"-wide seam allowance of fabric around the outside edge of the freezer paper.

Heart template for basting practice

Hearts

1. Thread a needle with an 18" length of thread. Do not knot one end as you normally would for basting. This makes it easier to remove the basting thread later.
2. Begin turning under the straight edge of the heart. To anchor the first stitch, take a few small stitches in place.

Baste the heart along the straight edge, turning under the seam allowance of the heart. Stop basting just before you reach the point of the heart.

3. To prepare the outside point, first turn the point of the fabric in toward the appliqué. Apply a small dab of glue stick to hold this in place. Fold the right side under, then the left, to form a sharp point.

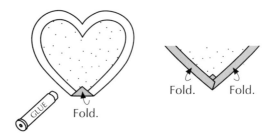

The seam allowances may overlap slightly at the point. They will overlap more on a very sharp point. If the point is too thick where the seam allowances cross, trim some of the seam width away, or push the extra fabric under the point with your needle later as you sew. Baste close to the edge.

Another method for basting outside points is to turn one side, then the other. A small tab of fabric may show, but you can tuck it under with your needle as you appliqué.

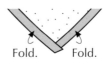

4. Continue basting the straight area of the heart until you come to the first curve at the top of the heart. As you baste the curve, ease the seam allowance around the curve. Do not clip the outside curve, as it will result in little bumps along the edge of the appliqué.

(continued on page 12)

Basting Practice Continued

If your seam allowance is wider than ¼", it helps to trim it around the curve to a "skimpy" ¼" (more accurately, ³⁄₁₆"). As you baste around the curve, keep your basting stitches small. Sew near the fold to keep the shape accurate.

If little points appear along the curve, you can push these under with the tip of your needle when you sew the appliqué to the background.

Another method for basting a curve is to take small running stitches in the seam allowance *only*, as you approach the curve. Do not baste through the paper and the right side of the appliqué fabric. Gently pull the thread to gather the fabric and ease it around the curve. This works especially well when appliquéing the basket in the "Welcome to Baltimore" quilt.

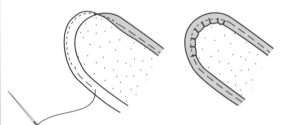

5. As you finish basting the first curve, you will come to the inside point. Carefully clip the seam allowance so that the fabric will turn under easily. Do not clip all the way into the appliqué design. Stop clipping about two threads out from the freezer-paper edge.

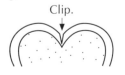

Clip.

As you baste the inside point, use smaller basting stitches, but do not force the threads at the point to turn under. These will be pushed under with the tip of the needle as you sew. Tack down the seam allowance edges, taking one stitch down away from the inside point. This method will prevent fraying at the inside point.

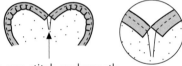

Take one stitch underneath and away from the point.

6. After basting the inside point, baste the second curve at the top of the heart, then overlap the beginning of your basting stitches along the straight edge. Don't tie a knot so that your basting threads can be removed easily.

Swags

The only basic shape not included in the heart shape is the inside curve. Inside curves, like the ones at the top of the swags in the "Welcome to Baltimore" quilt on page 33, need to be clipped in several places so that the seam allowance will turn under smoothly. Clip only halfway through the seam allowance to avoid fraying at the edge of the appliqué.

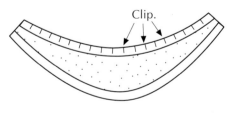

Clip.

Method One:
Traditional Appliqué

When I first learned to stitch appliqués, this is the method I used. You don't need any special tools, just fabric and thread!

1. Make a plastic template for the appliqué shape and trace the design onto the *right side* of your appliqué fabric.

Right side of fabric

2. Cut out the fabric shape, *adding a ¼"-wide seam allowance* all around.

3. Turn under the seam allowances, rolling the traced line to the back of the appliqué piece so it doesn't show on the front or along the edge of the appliqué.

4. Hand baste the seam allowance in place, using light-colored thread in the needle. See "Basting Practice" on pages 11–12 to learn how to turn straight and curved edges and how to treat inside and outside points.

5. Do not turn under edges that will be covered by other appliqué pieces. Each of these should lie flat under the appliqué piece that covers it.

6. Pin or baste the appliqué to the background fabric. Stitch the appliqué in place, using the "Traditional Appliqué Stitch" on page 18 or the "Ladder Stitch" on page 19.

Method Two:
Glue-Stick Preparation

You can substitute glue basting for hand basting, using a water-soluble glue stick. Using glue saves time when preparing the pieces for appliqué and washes out after the stitching is finished. Be sure to prewash your fabrics (page 6) if you choose this method.

1. Make a plastic template for the appliqué shape and trace the design onto the *right side* of your appliqué fabric.

2. Cut out the fabric shape, *adding a ¼"-wide seam allowance* all around.

3. Apply glue stick to the seam allowance on the wrong side of the appliqué. Try not to get too much glue in the fold area of the seam allowance or it will make the edges stiff and difficult to stitch in place.

Glue stick

4. Wait a few seconds for the glue to get tacky, then carefully fold the seam allowance to the back of the appliqué piece.

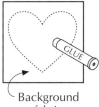

Fold.

5. Do not turn under edges that will be covered by other appliqué pieces. These should lie flat under the appliqué piece that covers it.

6. Baste the appliqué to the background fabric with glue. Apply glue to the background fabric in the center of the appliqué location. Position the appliqué on the background fabric, finger-press into place, and allow the glue to dry.

Background fabric

7. Stitch the appliqué in place, using the "Traditional Appliqué Stitch" on page 18 or the "Ladder Stitch" on page 19.

8. When you are finished stitching, soak the appliqué in warm, soapy water to remove the glue. After the piece is dry, press from the wrong side.

Method Three:
Needle-Turn Appliqué

This appliqué method moves right to the appliqué stitch. It saves time because you do not baste the seam allowances.

1. Make a plastic template for the appliqué shape and trace the design onto the *right side* of your appliqué fabric.

2. Cut out the fabric shape, *adding a skimpy ¼"-wide seam allowance* (³⁄₁₆" is the true measurement, but it's easier to remember "skimpy quarter-inch").

3. Position the appliqué piece on the background fabric and pin or baste it securely in place. Place the appliqué as accurately as possible, as the seam allowances will overlap the background markings.

4. Beginning on a straight edge, use the tip of your needle to gently turn under the seam allowance, about ½" at a time. Hold the turned seam allowance firmly between the thumb and first finger of one hand as you stitch the appliqué securely to the background fabric. Repeat the needle-turn and stitching steps as you work your way around the piece.

TIP

A longer needle, a milliner's or straw needle, will help you control the seam allowance and turn it under neatly. A round wooden toothpick will also help you turn under the seam allowance.

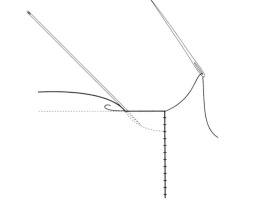

Method Four: Freezer-Paper Preparation

This has become my favorite method! Use freezer paper to help you make perfectly shaped appliqués. The paper sticks to the fabric and controls the shape. This technique improves accuracy in repeated designs. You can trace around a plastic template or simply trace the design onto the freezer paper. Be sure to prewash your fabrics (page 6) if you choose this method.

1. Place the freezer paper, *shiny side down*, on your pattern and trace the design using a sharp pencil. For pattern shapes that are asymmetrical, trace a reverse image of the design (page 9).

2. Carefully cut out the freezer-paper design on the pencil line. *Do not add seam allowances on the freezer paper*.

3. Place the shiny side of the freezer paper against the *wrong side* of the appliqué fabric and iron it in place, using a hot, dry iron.

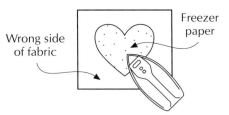

Wrong side of fabric

Freezer paper

4. Cut out the appliqué, *adding a ¼"-wide seam allowance* of fabric around the outside edge of the freezer paper.

5. Turn the ¼"-wide seam allowance toward the freezer paper and baste by hand or use a glue stick to baste it to the paper. Clip any inside points and fold the outside points.

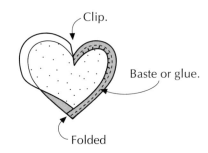

Clip.

Baste or glue.

Folded

6. Pin or baste the appliqué to the background fabric. Stitch the appliqué in place, using the "Traditional Appliqué Stitch" on page 18 or the "Ladder Stitch" on page 19.

7. After stitching the appliqués in place, remove the basting stitches. Cut a small slit in the background fabric behind the appliqué and remove the freezer paper with tweezers.

If you have basted with a glue stick, soak the piece in warm water for a few minutes to soften the glue and release the paper. Pull out the paper. After the appliqué dries, press it from the wrong side.

Method Five: Needle-Turn Freezer Paper

This technique uses freezer paper for accurate shaping but eliminates the basting step.

1. Trace the design onto freezer paper and cut it out on the pencil line. *Do not add seam allowances* on the freezer paper.

2. Iron the freezer-paper shape to the *wrong side* of the appliqué fabric.

3. Cut around the freezer paper, *adding a skimpy ¼"-wide seam allowance* of fabric around the outside edge of the freezer paper. Clip any inside corners, but do not turn under and baste the seam allowances to the wrong side of the appliqué.

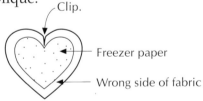

Clip.

Freezer paper

Wrong side of fabric

4. Position the appliqué piece on the background fabric and pin or baste it securely in place. Place the appliqué as accurately as possible, so that the seam allowances will overlap the background markings.

5. Beginning on a straight edge, use the tip of your needle to gently turn under the seam allowance, about ½" at a time. Hold the turned seam allowance firmly between the thumb and first finger of one hand as you

stitch the appliqué to the background fabric. Repeat the needle-turn and stitching steps as you work your way around the piece.

A longer needle, such as a milliner's or straw needle, will help you control the seam allowance and turn it under neatly. The stiffness of the freezer paper makes it easy to turn under the seam allowances and gives you a smooth, firm edge to work against. The result is a perfectly shaped finished appliqué.

6. After stitching the appliqués in place, cut a small slit in the background fabric behind the appliqué and remove the freezer paper with tweezers.

Method Six: Freezer Paper on Top

If you do not like the idea of cutting the back of your work to remove the freezer paper, try ironing the freezer-paper heart to the right side of your appliqué fabric. This method takes a little practice but it is fast and easy because there is no basting!

1. Trace the appliqué design onto freezer paper and cut it out on the pencil line. Iron the freezer-paper shape to the *right side* of the appliqué fabric. Cut out the appliqué, *adding a ¼"-wide seam allowance* around the outside edge of the freezer paper.

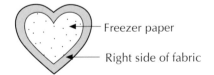

Freezer paper

Right side of fabric

2. Securely baste or pin the appliqué to the background fabric.

3. Following the shape of the paper, use the tip of your needle to gently turn under the seam allowance as shown for traditional needle-turn appliqué (Method Three, pages 13–14).

Turn under the seam allowance at the edge of the freezer paper so that the fabric is folded just beyond the edge of the freezer paper. Use the tip of the needle to smooth the fabric along the edge, then stitch the appliqué to the background fabric. Do not catch the paper in the stitching.

4. Peel away the freezer paper when you are finished. You can reuse these freezer-paper shapes several times.

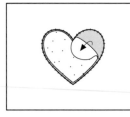

TIP

For perfect appliqué circles, you can use precut "office dots," which are available in a variety of sizes. They adhere to your fabric as you needle-turn around the shape. You can also cut appliqué shapes from self-stick labels—they stick well and can be reused several times.

Method Seven: Machine-Outlined Appliqué

Use this machine method to control fraying fabric on inside points. As you hand stitch the design to your background fabric, turn the machine stitches under at the edge of the appliqué to create a perfect shape.

1. Trace the appliqué design onto freezer paper and cut it out on the pencil line.

2. Iron the freezer-paper shape to the *right side* of the appliqué fabric. The freezer paper helps to stabilize your fabric as you sew and can be reused several times for this technique.

3. Using thread that matches the appliqué fabric, set your sewing machine for 15 to 20 stitches per inch. Sew around the outside edge

of the paper, overlapping the stitches at the end. Do not catch the paper in the stitching.

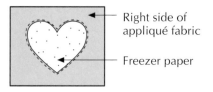
Right side of appliqué fabric
Freezer paper

4. Peel away the freezer paper. Cut out the shape, *adding a skimpy ¼"-wide seam allowance* beyond the machine stitches.

5. Pin the appliqué to the background fabric.

6. Using the tip of your needle as shown for traditional needle-turn appliqué (Method Three, pages 13–14), turn under the seam allowance until the machine stitches disappear. The machine stitches create a ridge along the outside edge of the appliqué. This ridge will help you keep the piece shaped accurately as you stitch.

7. Appliqué the design onto the background fabric. When you get to an inside point, clip the seam allowance all the way (but not through!) to the machine stitches. The small machine stitches will keep the fabric from fraying.

Method Eight: Double Appliqué

With this method, you use a double layer of fabric to create perfect shapes. The added layer gives a slightly padded appearance to your appliqué.

1. Cut two pieces of the appliqué fabric, making them slightly larger than your appliqué shape.

2. Trace the appliqué shape onto freezer paper. Cut out on the pencil line.

3. Iron the freezer-paper shape to the *wrong side* of one of the fabric pieces.

4. Place the fabric pieces right sides together

with the freezer paper facing you.

5. With your machine set for 15 to 20 stitches per inch, stitch completely around the edge of the paper design, overlapping the stitches where you started. Peel away the freezer paper.

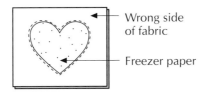

Wrong side of fabric

Freezer paper

6. Cut out the shape, *adding a slight ¼"-wide seam allowance* beyond the machine stitches. Clip corners and curves as needed.

7. Carefully make a small slit in the center of one layer of fabric. Turn the shape right side out through the slit.

8. Finger-press the seams flat along the edge, then press with a hot steam iron.

9. Pin the completed, double-layer appliqué to the background fabric, with the slit side against the background fabric.

10. Appliqué the design to the background, catching the top layer with your stitches.

Stitching Appliqués

Basting Appliqués to the Background

Before appliquéing, baste the appliqué pieces to the background fabric. Most stitchers pin-baste their appliqués in place, one or two pieces at a time. Use several pins to attach the appliqué pieces to the background so that they will not slip.

Small ¾" sequin pins are wonderful to use because they do not get in the way of the thread as you stitch.

> **TIP**
>
> *If you have trouble with threads tangling around pins as you sew, pin the appliqués in place from the wrong side of the background fabric.*

Hand basting is another option. This method is very secure. Use light-colored thread and position the basting stitches near the turned edges of the appliqués.

You may also baste the pieces in place using a water-soluble glue stick. Apply glue stick to the background fabric, keeping glue toward the center of the design.

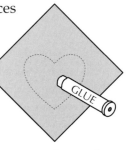

Do not apply glue along the outer edges where you will stitch, as it will stiffen the fabric and make it more difficult to sew the appliqué to the background. After applying the glue, position the appliqué and wait for the glue to dry before sewing. If you use a glue stick, you will need to wash the finished piece to remove the glue, so be sure to prewash your fabrics.

If you have a number of layers of appliqué pieces and the traced design on the background fabric is covered, you can position your appliqué pieces by making a pattern overlay. (See page 8.)

Layering Appliqué Pieces

As you organize for appliqué, take a moment to plan the sequence in which you will stitch the appliqués in place. Think about how things occur in nature as you plan an appliqué flower quilt. Stems grow first, then leaves appear, and finally buds and flowers. If your flowers are in a basket, vase, or pot, this is usually appliquéd first to hold the flowers.

For shapes that are layered, as the hearts are layered on top of the stars in "Wish Upon a Star" (page 43), the larger shape is appliquéd first, then the smaller shape on top. If you plan to quilt around the smaller shape, it helps to trim away the background fabric, leaving a ¼"-wide seam allowance, after you appliqué the larger shape. The remaining seam allowance will hold your appliqué securely!

If one shape overlaps another shape just slightly, stitch the shape that appears to be "cut off" first, then add the overlapping shape. For example, the "Miniature Violets" pot is stitched first, then the pot rim, then the leaves that overlap the edge of the pot. The top edges of the pot and rim do not have to be appliquéd because the raw edges will lie flat under other pieces.

The Traditional Appliqué Stitch

The traditional appliqué stitch is appropriate for sewing all areas of appliqué designs. It works well on straight areas as well as sharp points and curves.

1. Thread your needle with a single strand of thread approximately 18" long. Tie a knot in one end. To hide your knot, slip your needle into the seam allowance from the wrong side of the appliqué piece, bringing it out along the fold line. The knot will be hidden inside the seam allowance.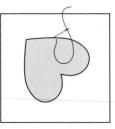

2. Stitch along the top edge of the appliqué. If you are right-handed, stitch from right to left. If you are left-handed, stitch from left to right. Start the first stitch by moving your needle straight off the appliqué, inserting the needle into the background fabric.

   Let the needle travel under the background fabric, taking a stitch parallel to the edge of the appliqué. Bring the needle up out of the background fabric about ⅛" away, along the pattern line. As you bring the needle back up, pierce the edge of the appliqué piece, catching only one or two threads of the folded edge.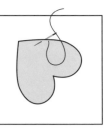

3. Then move the needle straight off the appliqué edge into the background fabric. Let your needle travel under the background, bringing it up about ⅛" away, again catching the edge of the appliqué. Give the thread a slight tug and continue stitching. The only visible parts of the stitch are small dots of thread along the appliqué edge.

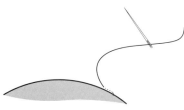

The part of the stitch that travels forward will be seen as ⅛" stitches on the wrong side of the background fabric. The length of your stitches should be consistent as you stitch along the straight edges. Smaller stitches are sometimes necessary for curves and points.

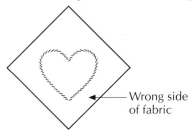

Wrong side of fabric

4. When you come to the end of your stitching or you are nearly out of thread, pull your needle through to the wrong side. Behind the appliqué piece, take two small stitches, making knots by bringing your needle through the loops.

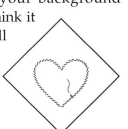

Before you cut your thread, take a moment to see if the thread will be shadowing through your background when you finish. If you think it will, take one more small stitch behind the appliqué to direct the tail of the thread under the appliqué fabric, then clip the thread.

The Ladder Stitch

The ladder stitch is another appliqué stitch that works well to appliqué straight areas and curves invisibly. When you stitch inside points or tight outside points, you may want to switch to the traditional appliqué stitch to create more durable stitches.

1. Thread your needle with a single strand of thread approximately 18" long. Tie a knot in one end. To hide your knot, slip your needle into the seam allowance from the wrong side of the appliqué piece, bringing it out through the fold line. The knot will be hidden inside the seam allowance.

2. Make a tiny stitch by moving your needle straight off the appliqué, inserting the needle into the background fabric. Travel along the pattern line under the background fabric about ⅛" and then bring the needle out.

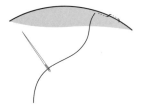

3. Insert the needle into the appliqué directly across from where you brought the needle out of the background. Travel through the fold of the appliqué about ⅛" and bring the needle out.

4. Move straight off the appliqué and take another stitch in the pattern line on the background fabric. Repeat until you have five or six stitches between the appliqué and the background fabric. The visible stitches will resemble the rungs on a ladder.

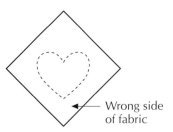

Pull lightly on the thread until the stitches disappear, attaching the appliqué neatly and invisibly to the background. The wrong side of your work will look like a running stitch, a series of stitches and spaces.

Wrong side of fabric

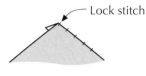

Stitching Practice

Practice stitching the edges of a heart-shaped appliqué. Use the template on page 11 to baste a heart and then stitch it to a small piece of background fabric. With this simple shape, you can practice on straight edges, outside points, outside curves, and inside points.

Stitching Straight Edges

Straight edges are the easiest to appliqué, so this is a good place to start practicing your stitches. Try to keep them even, straight, and consistent. Each stitch should be the same length, approximately ⅛" long.

Stitching Outside Points

As you stitch toward the outside point, make your stitches slightly smaller. Start taking smaller stitches within ½" of the point. If the seam allowance is too thick, you may need to trim the seam allowance or push the excess fabric under the point with the tip of your needle. Smaller stitches near the point keep any frayed edges of the seam allowance from escaping.

At the point, place your last stitch on the first side very close to the point. Place the next stitch on the second side of the point. A stitch on each side, close to the point, will accent the outside point. Do not put a stitch directly on the point, as that will flatten it.

If you have basted your point and a small tab of seam allowance is exposed, use your needle to push it under the appliqué before you stitch. If the exposed tab is on the second side of the point, take one extra "lock" stitch in place on the first side before you change directions at the point. This stitch will hold your fabric securely as you adjust the fabric on the second side.

Lock stitch

Stitching Outside Curves

As you stitch around the top of the heart, the shape of the curve becomes very round. Use the tip of your needle to arrange the fabric along the curve as you sew. To keep little points of fabric from sticking out, push the seam allowance under with the tip of your needle, smoothing it out along the folded edge before sewing. Keep your stitches fairly small so that these fabric points cannot escape between the stitches.

Stitching Inside Points

As you stitch toward the inside point, make your stitches smaller within ½" of the inside point of the heart.

Before you stitch the inside point, sweep any loose threads under the point. Insert the tip of your needle ½" past the point and gently sweep the needle back to the point, pushing any frayed threads under the appliqué. You can control the threads, using the tip of the needle with a dab of glue from a glue stick. A wooden toothpick will also help you sweep under any "fuzzies."

Take one stitch past the point, then return to add one extra stitch to emphasize the point. Come up through the appliqué, catching a little more fabric in the point—four or five threads instead of one or two. Make a straight stitch outward, inserting the needle under the point to pull it in a little and emphasize its shape.

If an inside point frays, use a few closely spaced stitches to tack the fabric down securely. Use thread that matches the appliqué fabric, so that these stitches will blend in with the edge of the shape.

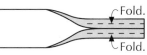

Appliquéing Special Shapes

Stems

There are several methods for creating stems for appliqué. If the stems are straight, they can be cut on the straight grain of the fabric. Curved stems must be cut on the bias.

Method One

This method is especially good for narrow stems.

1. Determine how wide the finished stem should be and cut strips four times the finished width.
2. Fold the strip in half lengthwise, *wrong sides together*. Press with a steam iron or baste close to the raw edges.

Fold.

3. Cut pieces from the strips for the stems. Cut them the measurement of the finished stem plus a ¼"-wide seam allowance on each end to layer under other appliqué pieces.
4. Position the raw edges of the stem just inside one of the marked stem lines. If the stems must curve, as in a wreath shape, position the raw edges of the strip just inside the outer (longer) curved line.

    Using small running stitches, sew the strip to the background through the center of the strip. (Actually stitch slightly toward the raw edges.) Backstitch every few stitches to secure the stem to the background.

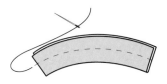

5. Roll the folded edge over the seam allowance. Appliqué the fold to the background fabric to create a smooth, even stem.

Method Two

These neatly basted strips are great for wider stems.

1. Cut strips that are twice the desired finished stem width.
2. Fold the raw edges in to meet in the center, *wrong sides together*. Baste along the folded edges, using small running stitches.

Fold.

Fold.

3. Cut pieces from the strips for the stems. Cut them the measurement of the finished stem plus a ¼"-wide seam allowance on each end to layer under other appliqué pieces.
4. Pin or baste the stems to the background fabric and appliqué along both folded edges. On a sharp curve, stitch the inside edge first, then the outside edge.

Method Three (Celtic Method)

You can use heat-resistant pressing bars, such as Quilters Press Bars, bias bars, or Celtic™ bars to make stems of a uniform width. These are available at quilt shops in several sizes, from ⅛" to ½" wide. Choose the size that matches the finished width of the stems in your design.

1. Determine how wide the finished stem should be and cut *bias* strips twice this width plus ½" for seam allowances.
2. Fold the strip in half lengthwise, *wrong sides together,* and machine stitch a scant ¼" from the raw edges to make a tube. Slip the Bias Bar into the tube and position it with the seam centered on one side of it. Press the tube flat, with the seam allowance to one side. If necessary, trim the seam allowance so it does not extend past the folded edge of the strip.

3. Remove the bar. Cut the tube into the required lengths for stems.
4. Position the stem on the background fabric, with the seam allowance next to the background. Pin or baste it to the background fabric and appliqué along both folded edges. On curved areas, use a steam iron to shrink out

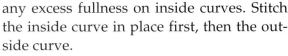

any excess fullness on inside curves. Stitch the inside curve in place first, then the outside curve.

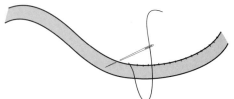

Leaves

The curved edges of leaves are easier to baste and stitch if the leaf is cut out on the bias. The bias edge will ease and create a smooth shape.

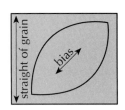

Treat sharp points on leaves as you would outside points as shown on page 11. Turn the point in toward the leaf, then fold the two sides in to form the point. Trim excess seam allowance to eliminate bulky points.

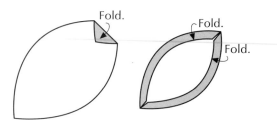

As you baste along curves, keep the stitches close to the fold to keep the shape accurate.

As you appliqué the leaves, place stitches on either side of the point to emphasize it.

If a leaf is connected to a stem or flower, begin stitching at the intersection. Take one or two stitches from the leaf to the stem so that they appear to be attached. The leaves and stems are not usually overlapped.

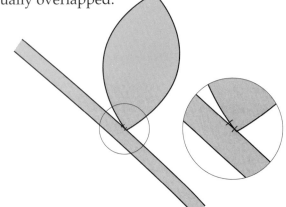

Three-Dimensional Buds

To make a folded bud, cut a 1¾" square of fabric. Fold the square diagonally, wrong sides together.

Fold each side point down to the center point, overlapping the points so they are about ¼" from the bottom point. Baste along the bottom edges of the bud.

If necessary, trim the raw edges of the bud so that it will fit within the markings for the calyx (base of the bud). Baste the bud within the calyx seam allowance. Let the bud edges remain free as you appliqué the calyx over the raw edges of the bud. Make sure you take a few stitches through the bud fabric to secure it inside the calyx.

Layered Tulips

Appliqué the center of the tulip first, stitching only the top edge. The sides of the tulip center will lie under the tulip petals. It helps to baste the loose edges to hold them in place as you stitch the petals.

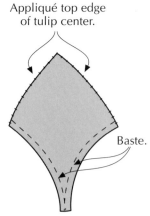

As you stitch the petals, make sure they cover the seam allowances of the tulip center. Begin stitching the second petal at the base, taking one or two stitches to connect the petals.

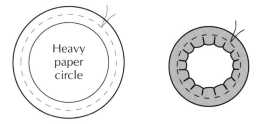

Posies

As you prepare your appliqué pieces, clip the inner points and inner curves on the posies so that the seam allowance will turn under easily. Carefully clip to within two or three threads of the inner point to eliminate "fuzzies" between the petals.

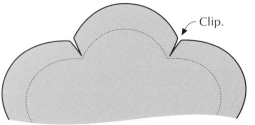

Clip.

Baste the posies to the background fabric, making sure they are securely layered over any stems they cover. Add perfect circles (below) for flower centers.

As you appliqué, use the tip of your needle to push under the threads and take tiny stitches at the inner points to control the threads.

If you plan to quilt around the center circle, it helps to trim away the background fabric behind the flower, leaving a ¼"-wide seam allowance.

Perfect Circles (for Flower Centers)

1. From heavy paper, such as a manila folder, cut circular templates the exact size of the finished circle. A plastic Circle Template, available in quilt shops or art stores, makes it easy to draw perfect circles.
2. Trace around the template onto the fabric. Cut fabric circles, adding ¼" around the edge of the circles.
3. Sew with a small running stitch around the fabric circle. Keep the stitches within the seam allowance but not too close to the edge.

4. Place the paper template in the center of the fabric circle. Pull the thread ends to draw the seam allowance in around the template.

Heavy paper circle

5. Steam-press the circle, then let it cool a minute. Carefully peel back the fabric and remove the paper circle. Gently pull the basting threads to tighten the seam allowance and make it lie flat. Tie a knot and trim the threads.
6. Pin the circle to the center of your flower, or the desired location, and appliqué with smaller-than-usual stitches.

For impressively small stitches, sew around the circle twice. The second time, place your stitches between the first ones.

Swags

1. Turn under the ¼"-wide seam allowance on the top and bottom edges of each swag. It is not necessary to turn under the ends of the swags because the raw edges will be covered by other appliqué pieces.

Raw edge

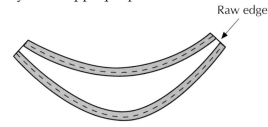

2. Appliqué the swag to the background fabric, using your favorite appliqué stitch.

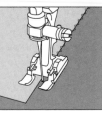

Invisible Machine Appliqué

If you have admired hand appliqué but felt it was too difficult or too time-consuming to add to your quilting repertoire, you will enjoy using Roxi's Smoothstitch™ technique to do machine appliqué that looks like it was done by hand. Roxi has perfected this machine-appliqué technique to make it more invisible and more secure than other methods. The results will amaze you! Not only will your appliqué look as though it were hand stitched, but it will also take a lot less time than hand appliqué.

Step-by-step directions for two methods of preparing appliqués (plus a special beginners' technique) are included in this section, along with instructions for sewing, cutting multiple pattern pieces, and adapting other patterns to this technique. It is easy to adapt Smoothstitch techniques to almost any appliqué pattern.

Fabrics

Choose fabrics made of 100% cotton. They are easier to handle than cotton/polyester blends. It is often difficult to turn a smooth edge with a blend. I have found very few fabrics, however, that will not work with this method. For additional information on selecting fabrics for appliqué, see pages 5–6.

Machine appliqué stitching is at its most invisible on printed fabrics. If you intend to use a solid-colored fabric, do a test strip to be sure you like the results. (See "The Basic Sewing Directions," step 2, on page 29.)

Prewash all fabrics to eliminate the possibility of shrinkage and of dyes running. If using Appliqué Preparation—Method II on pages 27–28, you must dampen the fabric to remove the paper. This may cause color bleeding even if your fabric has been prewashed. To be safe, do a test block.

Supplies and Tools

Sewing Machine

Machine appliqué requires a zigzag sewing machine that is in good working order.

Needle and Thread

Start with a sharp, new, size 70/10 or 60/9 needle in your machine. For nearly invisible machine-appliqué stitches, thread your machine with extra-fine, .004, invisible nylon machine quilting thread on top. Use cotton-covered polyester thread or 3-ply, mercerized cotton thread, size 50, in the bobbin. If you have tension difficulties with your machine, such as bobbin thread showing on top after all adjustments have been made (page 29), use a finer thread in your bobbin. Try serger thread or fine machine-embroidery thread.

Presser Foot

Use an open-toe appliqué foot for a clear, unobstructed view of the appliqué edge as you stitch.

Freezer Paper

Use freezer paper (plastic coated on one side) for appliqué pattern pieces. Your local quilt shop may carry a similar product for this purpose.

Pencils

Use only a pencil, never a pen, for tracing patterns onto the freezer paper. Make sure it is sharp or use a mechanical pencil.

Iron

Try using a small travel-size iron for preparing appliqué pieces. It is so lightweight that your wrist and arm won't get tired. Place the temperature setting on WOOL. Press over a piece of the nylon

thread to be sure it doesn't melt. If it does, lower the temperature. You don't want to "unstitch" all of your beautiful work.

Ironing Board

Use an ironing board with a firm surface for the best results, especially when preparing the appliqué pieces in Method I. If it is too soft, work on a flannel-covered board or a piece of firm, smooth-surfaced cardboard.

Glue Stick

When using a glue stick, be sure it's fresh. Keep the cap on when not in use so it doesn't become gummy.

Smoothstitch Appliqué Preparation

There are three ways to prepare appliqué pieces before stitching them to the background fabric.

Beginners' Method: This technique combines a little of Method I and Method II and is the recommended method if you've never worked with freezer-paper appliqué.

Method I: This technique is best for simple shapes, such as hearts, leaves, or swag border pieces.

Method II: Use this method for tiny or complex shapes that have tight curves and require a lot of clipping.

Beginners' Method

If you have struggled with freezer-paper appliqué in the past or if you have never tried it, I encourage you to try this method, using the heart appliqué shape on page 11.

1. Fold a piece of freezer paper in half with the shiny, coated side in. Trace the pattern onto one side. Staple and cut through *both* layers to get two freezer-paper pieces per appliqué. This gives you a mirror image (the side not traced on), plus the true pattern.

2. With your iron set on WOOL, no steam, press the mirror-image piece of freezer paper, *shiny side down*, to the *wrong side* of a piece of fabric. Cut out the fabric appliqué piece, *adding a ¼"-wide seam allowance* of fabric around the outside edge of the freezer paper.

3. Position the other freezer-paper piece, *shiny side up*, on top of the mirror-image piece you just ironed to the fabric. Place uncoated side to uncoated side. Glue the two together with a few dabs from your glue stick, just enough to hold the top one in place.

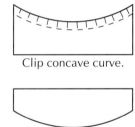

Position on top and glue in place.

Clip corners where needed, to within one or two threads of the paper. Clip concave curves (never convex curves), being careful not to clip all the way to the paper. The more clips, the smoother the curve.

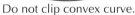

Clip concave curve.

Do not clip convex curve.

4. Use the tip of the iron to press the appliqué seam allowance onto the shiny side of the paper.

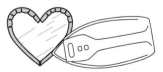

Remember to work on a firm surface. (See "Ironing Board" above.) Apply pressure to make the fabric adhere to the paper. If you accidentally press in a tuck that creates a point where the edge should be smooth, gently loosen the seam allowance from the paper and press again, redistributing the fullness of the fabric.

If your pattern has 90° corners or sharp points, secure loose corners with a small dab of glue from the glue stick. Do not trim the corners.

5. Continue with Appliqué Preparation—Method I, step 6, on page 27.

The advantage of this method is that you have a stiffer paper edge to press against and the fabric won't shift as you work with it. The disadvantage is that you need twice as many freezer-paper pieces.

Appliqué Preparation—Method I

This method is best for uncomplicated appliqué shapes, such as hearts, simple leaves, or swag borders. With this method, you turn the appliqué seam allowances to the back onto the shiny, coated side of a freezer-paper pattern piece of the desired finished shape and size.

> **Note**
> *For Method I, consider the uncoated side of the freezer paper the same as the right side of the fabric.*

1. Position a piece of freezer paper, *shiny side down*, over the chosen appliqué design. Using a pencil, trace the shape(s) onto the freezer paper and transfer the number(s) that indicate the sewing sequence. *Do not add seam allowances.* Draw small arrows on each shape to indicate which edges are to be turned and pressed.

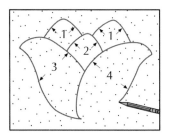

2. Carefully cut the traced pattern into individual pieces, making sure the edges are smoothly cut. If the edges are jagged, the finished appliqué edges will not be smooth. Place the freezer-paper pattern, *shiny side up*, on the *wrong side* of the fabric and pin.

TIP

Place pieces on the bias grain as much as possible since it's easier to turn under and shape edges with some bias stretch. This also eliminates some clipping of curves.

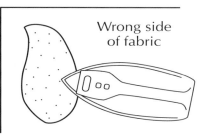
Wrong side of fabric

3. Cut out the appliqué piece, adding a ¼"-wide *seam allowance on all edges.*

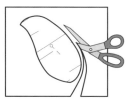
Add ¼" seam allowance all around.

4. Use the tip of the iron (dry iron, WOOL setting) to press appliqué seam allowances onto the shiny side of the freezer paper. Apply pressure to make fabric adhere to the paper.

5. Clip curves as needed for a smoothly turned edge, being careful not to clip all the way to the paper. If you accidentally press in a tuck that creates a point where the edge should be smooth, gently loosen the seam allowance from the paper and press again, redistributing the fabric fullness. *Do not press seam allowances under if they will be covered by another appliqué piece.*

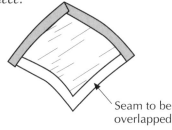
Seam to be overlapped

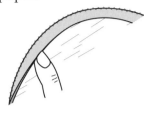

If the pattern has 90° corners or sharper points, secure loose corners with a small dab of glue from a glue stick. Do not trim the corners.

6. Notice that the shiny side of the freezer paper is exposed in the center of the appliqué. Position the appliqué, right side up, on the background fabric and fuse in place with a dry iron. Press until the plastic coating on the freezer paper softens and the appliqué adheres. If the appliqué is so small that very little freezer paper is exposed on the underside, use a small dab of glue to hold it in position.

Fuse in place on
background fabric.

7. Stitch appliqué in place, referring to "Attaching Appliqués," begining on page 29.
8. After each appliqué is stitched in place, remove the freezer paper, using one of the following methods:

    a. Reach under an unstitched edge of the appliqué, loosen the freezer paper from the seam allowance, and gently pull it out.

Loosen and remove
paper from the front.

OR

    b. Carefully cut away the background fabric behind the appliqué, leaving a ¼"-wide seam allowance of background fabric all around, inside the stitching.

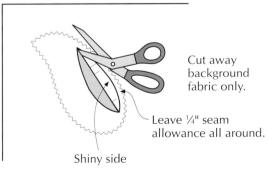

Cut away
background
fabric only.

Leave ¼" seam
allowance all around.

Shiny side

Gently loosen the fused seam from the freezer paper, using your fingernail, tweezers, an orange stick (from your manicure supplies), or the blade of a small screwdriver. Gently remove paper.

Appliqué Preparation—Method II

Use this method for more complex appliqué shapes. With this method, you fuse the freezer-paper pattern to the wrong side of the appliqué fabric, then turn and glue the appliqué edges to the uncoated side of the freezer-paper pattern.

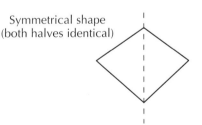

Note *For Method II, consider the shiny side of the freezer paper the same as the right side of the fabric.*

1. If the appliqué shape is symmetrical (both halves identical), use a pencil to trace it onto the freezer paper as directed in Method I.

Symmetrical shape
(both halves identical)

If the shape is asymmetrical (each half different), trace a reverse image onto freezer paper. *Do not add seam allowances.* Use arrows on each piece to indicate which edges to turn under.

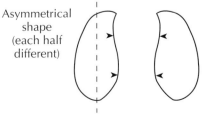

Asymmetrical
shape
(each half
different)

Reverse image

2. Carefully cut the traced freezer-paper pattern into individual pieces, making sure the edges are smoothly cut. (If the edges are jagged, the finished appliqué edges will not be smooth.)

3. Position the freezer-paper pattern, *shiny side down,* on the *wrong side* of the fabric. Fuse the paper to the fabric with the iron (dry iron, WOOL setting).

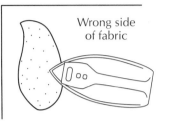

Wrong side of fabric

4. Cut the appliqué shape from the freezer paper–backed fabric, *adding a ¼"-wide seam allowance* all around. Clip curves and corners where necessary, being careful not to clip all the way to the paper pattern.

Clip corner.

5. Use a glue stick to apply a small amount of glue to the seam allowances. Fold them over onto the paper pattern and finger-press in place.

GLUE

TIP

For points with one flat side and one rounded side, glue the flat side down first. Then ease the rounder side onto freezer paper.

Press or glue flat side of point first.

6. Using a glue stick, apply a small amount of glue to the exposed freezer paper on the wrong side of the appliqué. Position appliqué, right side up, on the background fabric. If the appliqué is a fairly large piece, apply glue to the edges where fabric touches fabric. This

will prevent the background piece from shifting as you stitch.

7. Sew appliqué in place, referring to "Attaching Appliqués," beginning on page 29.

8. Remove the freezer paper after stitching each appliqué in place. Unless you can reach and remove the paper from the front as shown on page 27, carefully cut away the background fabric behind the appliqué, leaving a ¼"-wide seam allowance of background fabric all around the piece.

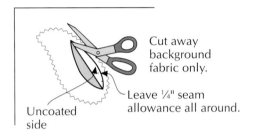

Cut away background fabric only.

Leave ¼" seam allowance all around.

Uncoated side

Spray the seam allowance area on the back side of the appliqué with water until wet but not dripping. Allow to sit for 7–10 minutes so the glue softens. Then, gently loosen the paper and slowly peel it away, using tweezers to get into tight spots. Allow to air dry before adding the next appliqué layer or carefully block and dry with your iron from the wrong side (or use a press cloth).

Transferring Appliqué Placement Lines

The quilt "Folk Flowers" (pages 48–50) includes the "Tulip Reel" block. The pattern for the block appears on page 62. The pattern has dotted lines that indicate center and diagonal lines. Adapt other appliqué designs that you wish to machine appliqué by adding these lines to the pattern to help you position the design accurately on the background fabric.

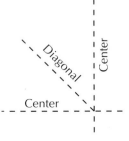

Diagonal

Center

Center

1. Fold the background fabric into fourths and finger-press the fold lines.
2. Unfold and lay the fabric over the master pattern, lining up folds and lines; pin.
3. Place on a light box or tape to a window to transfer the design onto the background fabric. (Directions for making a simple light box appear on page 8.) Trace over the lines only where two pieces touch each other. At other points of the design, mark ⅛" to ¼" inside the design lines.

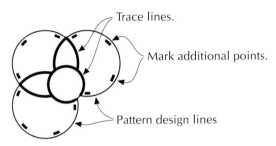

Trace lines.

Mark additional points.

Pattern design lines

Attaching Appliqués

The Basic Sewing Directions

1. Thread the sewing machine with regular thread on the top and in the bobbin and adjust the machine for a zigzag stitch 1mm to 1.5mm long (approximately 16 stitches per inch) and a little less than 1mm wide. Test the stitch for a balanced zigzag.
2. Thread the machine with invisible nylon, monofilament thread on top. In the bobbin, use cotton-covered polyester or mercerized cotton thread in a color that blends with the appliqué fabric. *Make a test strip to check your stitch and adjust tensions as needed.* To determine the correct tension, make this test strip consist of a background piece and a sample appliqué piece with freezer paper adhered to it. It may be necessary to loosen the top tension so the bobbin thread does not pull up to the top and show on the right side of your work. After loosening the top tension, make sure the bobbin thread still forms a zigzag stitch on the back.

On some machines, the bobbin case has a special eye for the bobbin thread to add extra tension. If your machine has this feature, thread the bobbin thread through the eye and test the stitch quality before adjusting the top tension.

Thread through special eye.

TIP *If you cannot adjust your machine enough to keep the bobbin thread from showing on top, try using serger thread or fine machine-embroidery thread in the bobbin.*

3. Position your work under the presser foot so the left swing position of the needle will stitch into the appliqué, and the right swing position will stitch into the background fabric just at the outer edge of the appliqué piece.

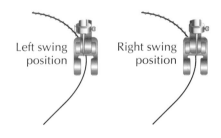

Left swing position

Right swing position

To lock the beginning and the end of the stitching, backstitch two or three stitches. (If tension and stitch width and length are set correctly, this will be very difficult to rip out!) Stitch slowly, since you are taking such tiny bites into the appliqué.

TIP *The most invisible stitch is narrow enough to catch only a few threads of the appliqué. All machines are different, but try halfway between .5 and 1mm.*

4. When approaching an inside corner, decrease the stitch length to almost 0 for the last few stitches before and after turning the corner.

This will create a tiny satin stitch in the corner. Return to the original stitch length and continue stitching.

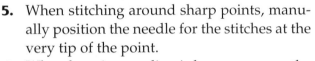

Satin stitch

Use the same technique for stitching around small, tight inside curves.

5. When stitching around sharp points, manually position the needle for the stitches at the very tip of the point.

6. When layering appliqué shapes, remove the freezer paper from each piece *after it is sewn in place and before adding the next layer on top*; reach under the unstitched edge of the appliqué to grasp it and pull it out. (If you forget to do this, you can cut away the background fabric as shown on page 27 and remove the paper from behind.)

7. Press completed appliqué from the back side, using the WOOL setting on the iron, or use a press cloth on top. *An iron that is too hot will melt the nylon thread holding the appliqués in place.* Press over a piece of the nylon thread to test the heat of the iron. The thread should be soft (not brittle) but should not melt. If necessary, lower the iron temperature.

Appliquéing Multilayered Designs

When appliquéing a multilayered design, you may appliqué the pieces together to create a unit.

1. Trace or photocopy your design onto a piece of typing paper. Photocopy at a very light setting to avoid carbon transferring onto your light fabrics.

2. Press prepared appliqué pieces to paper and stitch them to it, just as if it were the background fabric, stitching only where one appliqué touches another.

3. Gently tear away the typing paper, leaving the freezer paper intact. Appliqué the completed unit to the background around the outside edges only, then cut the background fabric away from behind to remove the paper.

The advantage to this method is that you can press all the pieces at once to the paper background. Also, it is easier when working on a large background piece, such as long border strips.

The only disadvantage is the need to tear the typing paper away from the stitching. Use tweezers to grasp and remove stray pieces of paper caught under the stitches.

Tube-Turning Stem Method

When your appliqué pattern calls for stems or narrow strips, it is important to cut them from the true bias so that you can shape them to curved areas of the design. You may cut and prepare the stems using one of the methods for hand appliqué shown on pages 21–22, or use the alternate method below.

1. Cut bias strips twice the desired finished width plus ½" for seam allowances. For example, for a ½"-wide finished strip, cut the bias strips 1½" wide. Sew strips together if necessary for the required length. To do this, trim the ends of the strips at a 45° angle and seam the ends to make a long, continuous strip. Press the seams open.

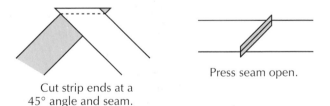

Cut strip ends at a 45° angle and seam.

Press seam open.

2. Fold each bias strip in half lengthwise, *right sides together*. Stitch ¼" from the raw edges.

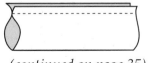

(continued on page 35)

Gallery of Quilts

A Year of Friendship by Mimi Dietrich, 1994, Baltimore, Maryland, 22½" x 27½". Twelve little designs, each one made for a month of the year, create a wonderful calendar designed by friends in the Catonsville Quilt and Tea Society. Setting designed by Diana Harper. Directions on page 52.

Button Baskets by Mimi Dietrich, 1994, Baltimore, Maryland, 22" x 22". Select one of the blocks from "A Year of Friendship" and make a special little quilt by repeating the design. Buttons were added to fill each basket. Baskets designed by Libbie Rollman.

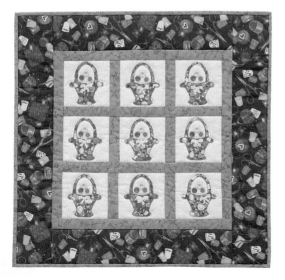

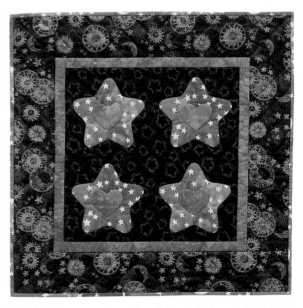

Wish Upon a Star by Mimi Dietrich, 1994, Baltimore, Maryland, 26½" x 26½". This is a great beginner's appliqué project. Celestial fabrics work well in this quilt. Don't forget to make a wish as you appliqué each heart! Directions on page 43.

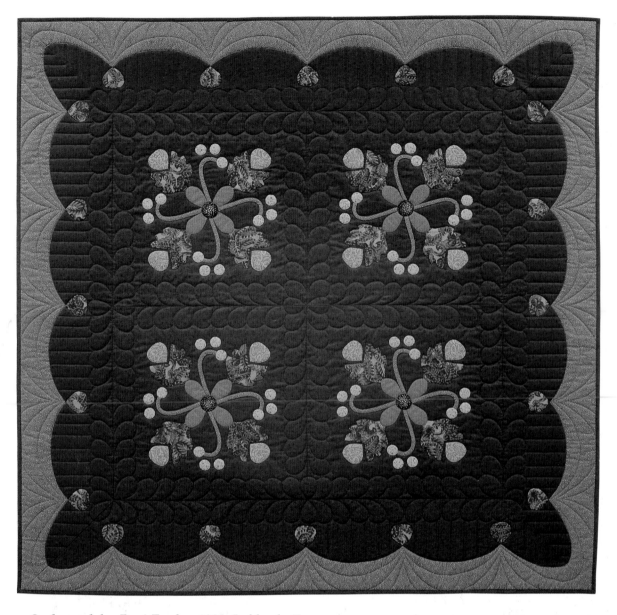

Cockscomb by Roxi Eppler, 1994, Lubbock, Texas, 50" x 50". An antique quilt owned by a friend inspired this design. Directions on page 50.

Miniature Violets by Mimi Dietrich, 1994, Baltimore, Maryland, 16½" x 16½". Even if you don't have a green thumb, you can "grow" these delightful violets, using dimensional appliqué techniques. Directions on page 46.

Welcome to Baltimore by Mimi Dietrich, 1994, Baltimore, Maryland, 31" x 31". Even though the blocks are different, each of the blocks in this album quilt contains the same flowers, buds, leaves, and hearts. Stitched together, they make an album of appliquéd designs. Directions on page 44.

Folk Flowers by Roxi Eppler, 1993, Lubbock, Texas, 34" x 34". Because of her love for primitive-style folk designs, Roxi created this sampler of flowers. Directions on page 48.

(continued from page 30)

3. Turn right side out, using a turning tool, such as Fasturn®. Press, keeping the seam on the underside of the tube you have created.

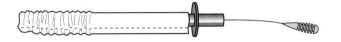

4. Use glue to position completed stems or strips on background fabric. Place a sheet of paper or removable stabilizer under the block and machine appliqué in place. Remove paper.

Adapting Appliqué Patterns

Appliqué shapes with sharp points and curves should be rounded out, so to speak. For easier stitching, sharp points and corners should be closer in shape to a 90° angle.

Expand tight curves as shown below.

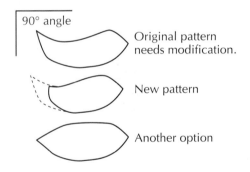

Turn one shape with a very sharp angle into two shapes with no angles.

See also "Design Tips" on pages 40–41.

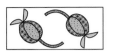

Note

You can also appliqué shapes with very sharp points. Turn and press the seam allowance along both edges of the point, accordion-fold the loose corner, and apply a little glue from a glue stick to each fold to secure it.

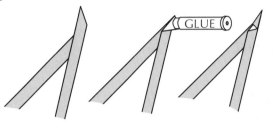

Accordion-fold and glue sharp points.

Cutting Multiple Appliqué Patterns

Some appliqué projects require pattern shapes that are used repeatedly. To make quick work of cutting symmetrical pattern shapes (both halves identical) in multiples, trace the pattern several times along one edge of a piece of freezer paper. Accordion-fold the paper to four thicknesses, with the designs still visible, and staple paper layers together inside each pattern outline. Carefully cut out pattern pieces.

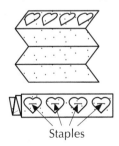

Staples

To cut multiples of pattern shapes that are asymmetrical (each half different), trace the pattern several times onto the uncoated side of a piece of freezer paper. Stack this piece on top of three additional layers of freezer paper, *shiny sides down,* and staple the layers together as before. Use enough staples to prevent shifting during the cutting process. Cut out the pattern pieces.

Cutting "Snowflake" Appliqué Patterns

You can use the Smoothstitch appliqué method to appliqué snowflake and Hawaiian-style motifs. Use the following technique to cut accurate freezer-paper shapes for this type of design.

1. Cut a square of freezer paper the size of the quilt block. Fold in half and finger-press the crease.

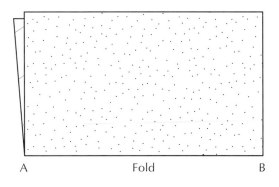

A　　　　　Fold　　　　　B

2. Fold in half again, bringing A and B together.

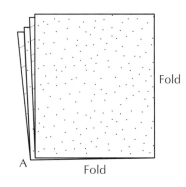

3. Unfold the freezer paper and place over the appliqué pattern, with the uncoated side facing up. Trace the design onto two adjacent quarters.

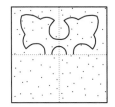

4. Fold in half and staple. Do not fold and cut more than two thicknesses, or your pieces may not be accurate.

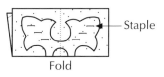

5. Cut out the appliqué shape and remove staples. Use Method II on pages 27–28 to cut and prepare appliqués.

Smoothstitch Appliqué as an Alternative to Curved Piecing

You can use this invisible machine-appliqué method to create blocks for a Drunkard's Path quilt, eliminating the tedious curved seaming that is typical of this traditional pieced design.

1. Appliqué circles to squares, using the appliqué preparation method of your choice.

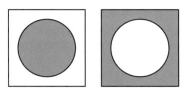

2. Cut each square into four quarters and reassemble the quarters to make a traditional Drunkard's Path or one of its many variations.

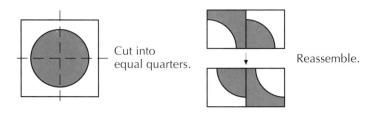

Fusible Appliqué

If you like the look of hand and machine appliqué but do not want to invest too much time in a wall hanging or other project that will not receive much wear, consider fusible appliqué. In addition to the fabrics for the background and the appliqués, you will need a paper-backed fusible web, such as Wonder-Under, HeatnBond, or Aleene's Fusible Web™.

Fusible webs are made of thermoplastic fibers that are adhered to a piece of release paper. When you place the web against the wrong side of a piece of fabric and apply the heat and pressure of an iron to the paper side for a few seconds, the web adheres to the fabric. When you remove the paper backing, you can permanently fuse the piece of fabric to another layer of fabric. When allowed to cool, the melted fibers of the web form a thin, permanent bond between the fabrics, which is desirable when doing machine appliqué as it eliminates slipping and puckering while you stitch the fabric shapes in place. The only disadvantage is that the fused shapes are a little stiffer than the two layers of fabric without the web between them.

For some fusible appliqué projects, you may simply cut and fuse the appliqué shapes in place on the background fabric. This is particularly appropriate for wall hangings. For a more durable and more decorative effect, use the web as a bonding agent so that you can hand or machine stitch easily and smoothly around the outer edges of the appliqués to make them more permanent. Depending on the stitch and the thread you choose, this stitching can be decorative or almost unnoticeable.

The Basic Fusing Directions

1. Position the fusible web over the appliqué pattern piece with the paper side up.

   Symmetrical designs are traced directly from the pattern to the paper. For asymmetrical designs, like the sunflowers in the "Folk Flowers" quilt on page 34, you must trace a reverse (mirror) image of the pattern piece. To trace a reverse image, turn the pattern over and place it on a light box or against a bright window. Or, accurately trace the design onto tracing paper, then turn the tracing paper over, lay your freezer paper on top (shiny side down), and trace the design.

Note
The asymmetrical designs for "A Year of Friendship" have already been printed in reverse for you.

2. Use a pencil to trace the appliqué shapes onto the paper.
3. Cut the appliqué shape from the fusible web, cutting just outside the marked line.
4. Place the shape, *fusible web side down*, on the *wrong side* of the appropriate appliqué fabric. Following the manufacturer's directions, fuse in place. Allow to cool before handling.

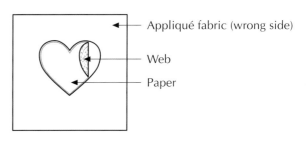

Appliqué fabric (wrong side)

Web

Paper

5. Cut out the shape on the drawn line. *Do not add seam allowances* to the edges of the shape.

6. Peel away the paper backing. If it is difficult to grasp the edge of the backing to tear it away, tug gently to make the paper rip so you can grasp a torn edge.

7. Arrange the fusible-backed appliqués in position on the right side of the background fabric and fuse in place, following the manufacturer's directions. Allow to cool before handling.

Stitching Fused Appliqués

To stitch fused appliqués by hand:

1. Depending on the look that you want to achieve, use two strands of embroidery floss in a color that matches the color of the appliqué, or use a contrasting-color thread that will show.

2. The "buttonhole stitch" or "blanket stitch" is a nice way to embellish the edges of your appliqués.

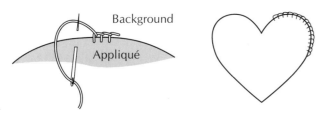

3. The "primitive stitch" is a simple straight stitch, placed perpendicular to the edges of the appliqué. Bring your needle up through the appliqué (about ⅛" in from the edge), then take a straight stitch off the edge into the background fabric.

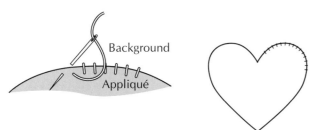

To stitch fused appliqués by machine:

1. Thread the machine with thread that matches the color of the appliqué. Replace the regular presser foot with an open-toe embroidery foot if available for your machine. (See illustration on page 24.)

2. Set the machine for a tiny satin stitch (short, narrow zigzag stitch). If you have adjusted the stitch correctly, it will be ⅟₁₆" to ⅛" wide and very closely spaced. Test the stitch on scraps and adjust the tension so it is slightly looser on top. Bobbin thread should not show on top.

3. Place the appliqué under the needle and satin-stitch over the raw edges. The right swing of the needle should penetrate the background fabric; the left swing of the needle should go through the appliqué. Make sure all raw edges of the appliqué are covered with stitches.

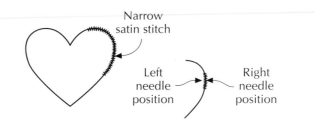

> **TIP**
>
> *Place a piece of tear-away stabilizer on the wrong side of your work (or iron a piece of freezer paper on the back) to prevent puckering while you stitch. Remove when you have completed all of your machine stitching.*

On some sewing machines, you can duplicate the look of hand blanket stitching. Consult your sewing machine manual or your dealer for details.

Machine Stitching Tips

When stitching around curves, stop every few stitches with the needle down in the fabric and lift the presser foot so you can turn the piece ever so slightly before taking the next few stitches.

When turning around points, try gradually decreasing the stitch width as you reach the point and then stitch away from it. Return the stitch to the original setting. Practice this adjustment on scraps first.

To stitch an outside corner with a secure overlapping zigzag:

1. Stitch the first side of the appliqué, ending at the outside corner with the needle in the background fabric at the outside edge of the appliqué.

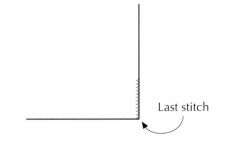

Last stitch

2. Raise the presser foot and rotate the fabric to a ready-to-stitch position; stitch. The first few stitches you take will overlap the stitches at the corner.

To stitch an outside corner with a mitered zigzag stitch that isn't quite as thick as the overlapped corner above:

1. Complete step 1 above.

2. Raise the presser foot, rotate the fabric halfway, and take one stitch over the previous stitches.

3. Raise the presser foot, rotate the fabric so you are ready to stitch the next side; continue stitching.

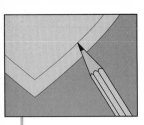

Hints from Mimi and Roxi

Design Tips

You can create your own appliqué designs! Here are a few of our hints to help you get started!

❑ Keep it simple! Draw the outline for a simple shape, such as a leaf. Let the fabric you choose add the extra lines, texture, and dimension to make your appliqué appear realistic.

❑ If you can't draw—trace! Trace on white paper, using a dark pencil or marker to make a neat appliqué pattern. Look all around you. Pick up a leaf or flower petal and trace around it to create a floral appliqué design.

Designs in a favorite book, greeting card, poster, or advertisement may also be used to create your own appliqué pattern. For a child's quilt, trace a favorite drawing from a child's book, coloring book, or wallpaper.

❑ Simplify the design by tracing only the outline of shapes, omitting unnecessary details. Eliminate excess parts of the design you are tracing. Combine three flowers into one, put one star in the sky instead of many, trace one teddy bear instead of a group. The fabrics and colors you choose for appliqué will add features and bring the appliqué back to life.

❑ If your design is not the size you want, enlarge or reduce your tracing with the use of a photocopy machine. If a design must be enlarged several times, the lines will become blurry. If this happens, take the time to retrace the design with neat clear lines.

❑ Think about the appliqué process as you create a design. Adjust the designs to match your appliqué skill level:

✓ Change a sharp point into a blunt point or even into a softly rounded curve.

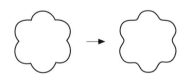

✓ Replace an inside point with a rounded curve.

✓ Instead of a deep inside point, substitute two appliqué pieces to avoid the deep point.

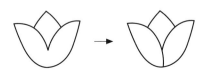

Sources of design inspiration: photographs, stamps, jewelry, cards, vases, flowers, magazines...

✓ Modify parts of a design to eliminate inside points. When two pieces overlap, it automatically creates a crisp inside point.

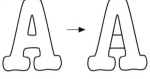

✓ Appliqué a separate leaf next to a stem instead of having them be one unit. This avoids a deep inside point.

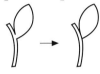

✓ As you plan your stitching, overlap pieces instead of butting them up against each other.

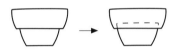

☐ Experiment with both traditional hand appliqué and machine appliqué techniques. For instance, even though we have included Mimi's hand appliqué techniques for making "Wish Upon A Star" (page 43), you could make it using fusible techniques or Roxi's Smoothstitch technique. And, there is absolutely no reason why you can't combine techniques!

☐ Don't be afraid to substitute design elements in appliqué patterns. In "Welcome to Baltimore" (page 44), replace the heart and posy in the wreath with tulips to create your own Tulip Wreath. In the "Folk Flowers" pattern, change the pomegranates to a primitive rose design. It's YOUR quilt! Make it fun and easy for you to stitch!

Quilt Finishing

For detailed directions for finishing your quilts, refer to *Loving Stitches* by Jeana Kimball and *Happy Endings* by Mimi Dietrich (That Patchwork Place). Included below are binding techniques that we use.

Mimi's Binding Basics

Binding adds the finishing touch to your quilt. It is usually a good idea to use one of your darker fabrics to frame your design.

1. Baste around the edge of your quilt to securely hold the three layers together. Trim any excess threads, batting, or backing even with the front of the quilt.

2. Measure the distance around your quilt and add 10". You will need this length of binding strips to finish your quilt. Cut enough 2"-wide strips of binding fabric across the 44" width of fabric. These can be cut quickly with a rotary cutter and a clear acrylic ruler.

3. Sew the strips together, using diagonal seams, to create one long strip of binding. To make diagonal seams the easy way, cross two strip ends at right angles, right sides together. Lay these on a flat surface and imagine the strips as a large letter "A." Draw a line across the crossed pieces to "cross the A," then sew along the line. Your seam will be exact, and you can unfold a continuous strip.

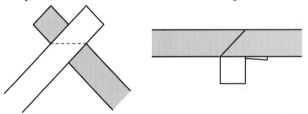

Trim off the excess fabric, leaving a ¼"-wide seam allowance.

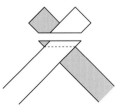

Press this seam open to distribute the thickness of the seam.

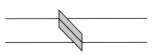

4. Fold the binding strip in half lengthwise, wrong sides together, and press with a hot steam iron.

5. Match the two cut edges of the binding strip to the front cut edge of the quilt. Start sewing the strip approximately 6" from one of the corners, using a ¼"-wide seam. For durability, sew this seam by machine.

6. To miter the corners of the binding, stop stitching ¼" from the corner and backtack.

Stop stitching ¼" from corner.

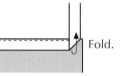

Fold the binding diagonally as shown so that it extends straight up from the second edge of the quilt.

Fold.

Then, fold the binding down even with the second edge of the quilt. The fold should be even with the first edge. Start sewing the binding ¼" from the fold, making sure to backtack.

Fold.

As you fold the corner to the back of the quilt, a folded miter will appear on the front.

Front

On the back, fold one side first, then the other, to create a miter on the back.

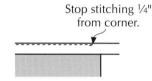

7. To connect the ends of the binding, allow the end to overlap the beginning edge by 2". Cut the end diagonally, with the shortest end of the diagonal on top, nearest to you. Turn the diagonal edge under ¼" and insert the beginning "tail" inside the diagonal fold.

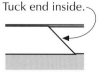

Tuck end inside.

Turn under ¼" on diagonal end.

Continue sewing the binding onto the quilt. When you turn this area to the back of the quilt, hand stitch the diagonal fold.

8. Fold the binding over the edge of the quilt. The folded edge of the binding should cover the stitching on the back of the quilt. Hand stitch the binding to the back of the quilt, using the traditional appliqué stitch.

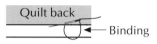

Quilt back

Binding

Roxi's Smoothstitch Binding

1. Prepare binding strips, following Mimi's directions that begin on page 41; however, in step 5, sew the binding to the *back side* of the quilt top. Continue through step 7.

2. Press the binding away from the quilt back so that it will be easier to turn to the front. Fold the binding over the edge of the quilt to the front of the quilt.

Press binding away from quilt back.

Quilt back

3. Place the walking foot on your machine. Pin each corner miter in place.

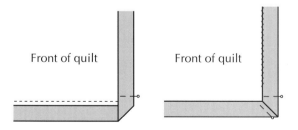

Front of quilt   Front of quilt

4. Smoothstitch the binding onto the front of the quilt as if it were an appliqué. You will have a zigzag stitch on the back side, so be sure to use a bobbin thread that will match your backing fabric.

The Quilts

Wish Upon a Star

Finished Quilt Size: 26½" x 26½"
Finished Block Size: 8" x 8"
Color photo on page 31

This project is designed especially for the beginner! The pieces are large and fun to appliqué. The stars are designed without sharp inner or outer points so that your stitches glide around the soft curves. Four hearts or "wishes" are added to give you practice with a few points. If this is your first hand-appliqué project, use the eight methods that begin on page 13 to prepare the stars and hearts. Once you have completed this quilt, you can go on to more difficult appliqué projects.

For those of you who are skilled at hand appliqué but haven't yet tried machine methods, this is a good first machine-appliqué project. Machine-appliqué methods begin on page 25.

Find some wonderful star fabric and make a wish as you appliqué each star!

Cutting

Use the templates on page 54.
▶ From the dark fabric, cut:
  4 squares, each 8½" x 8½", for background blocks
▶ From the print fabric, cut:
  4 Template #1 (stars)
  3 strips, each 2" x 42", for binding
▶ From the hand-dyed fabric, cut:
  4 Template #2 (hearts)
  2 strips, each 1½" x 16½", for inner side borders
  2 strips, each 1½" x 18½", for inner top and bottom borders
▶ From the outer border fabric, cut:
  2 strips, each 4½" x 18½", for outer side borders
  2 strips, each 4½" x 26½", for outer top and bottom borders
▶ From the backing fabric, cut a 32" x 32" square.

Appliquéing and Quilt Top Assembly

1. Fold each of the 4 background blocks in quarters to find the center point. Match this point to the center point of the pattern on page 54 and trace the star and heart onto each block.

2. Make appliqué templates for the heart and star. Cut and prepare the appliqué pieces from the appliqué fabrics. If you like, use different methods to prepare the pieces, so that you can practice each one.

3. Appliqué a star to each of the blocks. Trim away the background fabric behind each star, leaving a ¼"-wide seam allowance. (See page 27.)

4. Appliqué a heart to each star. In order to properly place each heart, make a pattern overlay as shown on page 8 or use the pattern to mark the centers of the star and heart with pins.

5. Sew the four squares to-gether, using ¼"-wide seam allowances.

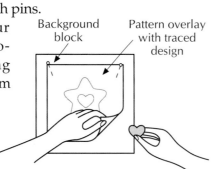

Background block

Pattern overlay with traced design

6. Sew the inner border strips to the sides and then to the top and bottom edges of the quilt top. Press seams toward the border.

7. Sew the outer border strips to the sides and then to the top and bottom edges of the quilt top. Press seams toward the border.

Quilt Finishing

Refer to *Loving Stitches* by Jeana Kimball and *Happy Endings* by Mimi Dietrich (That Patch-work Place) for more information about quilt-ing and finishing quilts.

1. Beginning in the corners and working toward the center of the quilt top, mark diagonal quilting lines on the background and border as shown. Mark the lines 1½" apart and do not mark lines through the appliqués.

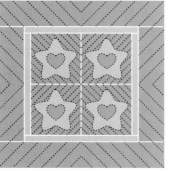

2. Layer the quilt top with batting and backing; baste.

3. Outline quilt around the hearts and stars and on either side of the inner border. Quilt on the marked diagonal quilting lines.

4. Bind the edges.

Welcome to Baltimore

Finished Quilt Size: 31" x 31"
Finished Block Size: 10" x 10"
Color photo on page 33

Block A   Block B

Block C   Block D

In the nineteenth century, women made appliquéd album quilts. The most famous album quilts were made in Baltimore, Maryland. Each block on the quilt was a different design, with the colors predominantly red and green. In this little Baltimore Album quilt, each block includes the same leaves, flowers, and buds. Stitch this yourself, or share the patterns with three friends and make a friendship album!

Materials: 44"-wide fabric

1⅜ yd. white-on-white print for background
¾ yd. red print for appliqués, inner border, and binding
½ yd. dark green print for appliqués
¼ yd. dark blue print for appliqués
¼ yd. light blue print for appliqués
¼ yd. gold print for appliqués
1 yd. for backing
34" x 34" square of batting

Cutting

▶ From the white-on-white print, cut:
  4 squares, each 10½" x 10½"*, for background
  4 strips, each 5½" x 33", for outer border
▶ From the red print, cut:
  2 strips, each 1" x 20½", for inner side border
  2 strips, each 1" x 21½", for inner top and bottom border
  4 strips, each 2" x 42", for binding
▶ Set aside the remaining fabrics.

*If you wish, you may cut the squares larger (12½") and trim them each to a 10½" square after completing the appliqués.

Appliquéing and Quilt Top Assembly

1. Fold each of the four background squares in quarters to find the center point. Match this point to the center point of the appliqué patterns on pages 55–58. Trace the four appliqué designs onto the background squares.
2. Referring to the quilt plan, trace the border designs from the pattern on page 59, onto pieces of paper, then tape the pieces of paper together to form one long pattern. Center the outer border strips over the design and trace the design onto the fabric. Wait until the quilt

is assembled to trace the corner designs.
3. Make appliqué templates for the blocks and border, using the patterns on pages 55–60. Cut and prepare the appliqué pieces from the appliqué fabrics, using your favorite method. See page 23 for preparing swags for appliqué.
4. Appliqué the designs to the blocks in numerical order, using your favorite stitching technique. Refer to page 22 for three-dimensional appliqué buds.
5. Appliqué the swags to the border strips, then the hearts.

6. Referring to the quilt plan, sew the four squares together, using ¼"-wide seam allowances. If you cut the background blocks oversize, trim them all to 10½" x 10½" squares, being careful to center the design in each block.
7. Sew the inner border strips to the sides and then to the top and bottom edges of the quilt top. Press seams toward the border.
8. Sew the outer border strips to the sides and then to the top and bottom edges of the quilt top. Carefully match the center of the border to the center of the quilt edge. Press seams toward the inner border.
9. Trace the corner designs in each corner, using the pattern on page 60. Appliqué the designs in numerical order.

Quilt Finishing

1. To mark the background quilting design, place dots at 1" intervals along the edges of the 10" x 10" blocks. Then use a long ruler and marking pencil to connect the dots with diagonal lines. Do not mark lines through the appliqués.

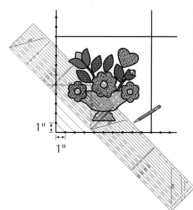

Repeat the process, making diagonal lines the opposite way to create a grid.

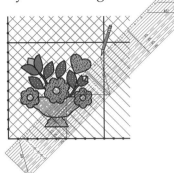

2. To mark the quilting lines in the outer border, draw lines 1" apart and radiating from each corner as shown on the border patterns on pages 59 and 60.
3. Layer the quilt top with batting and backing; baste.
4. Outline quilt around the appliqués and on both sides of the inner border. Quilt on the marked quilting lines.
5. Bind the edges.

Miniature Violets

Finished Quilt Size: 16½" x 16½"
Finished Block Size: 5" x 5"
Color photo on page 32

Even if you don't have a green thumb, you can "grow" beautiful violets! Take a step into another dimension with this "Miniature Violets" quilt. You can make the

leaves and violets using dimensional appliqué techniques that are fun, easy, and very realistic!

Search your fabric shops for the perfect violet fabric. Hand-dyed fabrics often have the mottled look you might like for the pots. If you can't find two "clay" fabrics for the pots, try using the right and wrong sides of one fabric!

Materials: 44"-wide fabric

¾ yd. white-on-white print for background, binding, and backing
⅛ yd. light clay-colored fabric for pots
⅛ yd. dark clay-colored fabric for pots
⅛ yd. green for leaves
½ yd. dark purple for violets and borders
¼ yd. light purple for borders
18" x 18" square of batting
Yellow seed beads

Cutting

Use the templates on page 61.
▶ From the white-on-white, cut:
   4 squares, each 5½" x 5½", for background
   2 strips, each 2" x 42", for binding
   1 square, 18" x 18", for backing
▶ From the dark purple fabric, cut:
   24 Template #2
   9 Template #3
   18 Template #4
   12 Template #6 (for gathered blossoms)
▶ From the light purple fabric, cut:
   12 Template #1
   36 Template #5

Appliquéing and Quilt Top Assembly

1. Trace the "Miniature Violets" design onto the four background squares, using the pattern on page 61.
2. Make freezer-paper templates for 4 pots, 4 pot rims, and 4 each of the leaves. See page 9 for making freezer-paper templates. Trace the dotted line in the center of each leaf and label each leaf.
3. Iron the freezer-paper templates to the wrong side of the "clay" fabrics for the pots and rims.

Appliqué the pot first, leaving the top edge of the pot unstitched since it will lie under the rim. Pull the freezer paper away from the appliqué.

4. Appliqué the rim in place, leaving the top edge unstitched where it will lie under the leaves. Pull the freezer paper away from the appliqué.

5. Create pinched leaves for a dimensional effect. On each marked freezer-paper leaf, cut a slit on the traced dotted line, from the base of the leaf to the outer edge, stopping just before you get to the tip.

6. Iron the freezer-paper leaf templates to the leaf fabric, spreading the base of the paper leaf ¼" apart. Cut out the fabric leaf with this extra fullness, adding a ¼"-wide seam allowance all around. Do not remove the freezer paper yet. Pinch the excess fabric in the center of the leaf to bring the paper edges back together.

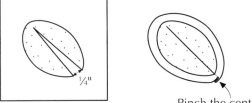

Pinch the center.

7. Appliqué the leaf edges to the marked lines on the background fabric. Remove the paper, then baste across the seam allowance to secure the pinched fabric. Appliqué the back leaves first, then the side leaves, and finally the front leaf.

8. To make the gathered blossoms, turn under ⅛" around the edge of each dark purple circle and secure with a running stitch near the fold. Gather the edges together in the center of the circle and tie a secure knot. If the edges do not meet tightly, take a few stitches back and forth to close the hole.

9. With the gathered side up, divide the edges of the flower into five equal sections as shown, marking lightly with a fabric marker.

10. Insert the needle straight down through the center of the gathers, bringing it through to the back side.

To make the petals, bring the thread from the back over the outside edge of the flower and insert it into the center again. Place the thread at one of the edge markings, then pull the thread to create a petal.

Continue looping the thread over the edges to create five petals.

Knot the thread on the back of the flower. Add three yellow beads to the center. Tack the violets to the marks on the leaves.

11. To make sashing strips, sew a dark purple piece 2 to each side of a light purple piece 1.

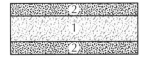

Make 12.

12. Sew a light purple piece 5 to each side of a dark purple piece 4. Sew the resulting triangles to each side of a dark purple piece 3, to make setting squares.

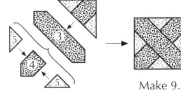

13. Sew 2 rows of sashing strips and appliquéd blocks together as shown.

Make 9.

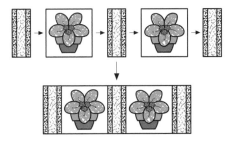

Make 2.

14. Sew 3 rows of sashing strips and setting squares together as shown.

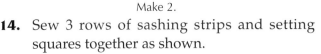

Make 3.

15. Sew the rows of appliquéd blocks and sashing strips together with the rows of setting squares and sashing strips as shown.

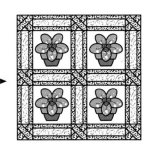

Quilt Finishing

1. Layer the quilt top with batting and backing; baste.
2. Quilt around the edges of the pots and leaves. Quilt in-the-ditch around the dark purple borders.
3. Bind the edges.

Folk Flowers

Finished Quilt Size: 34" x 34"
Finished Block Sizes: 7" x 16" and 8" x 8"
Color photo on page 34

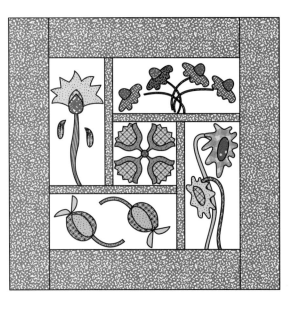

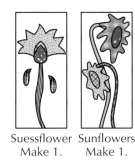

Suessflower   Sunflowers
Make 1.   Make 1.

Tulip Reel   Coneflowers
Make 1.   Make 1.

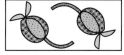

Pomegranates
Make 1.

Materials: 44"-wide fabric

½ yd. Fabric A for background
¾ yd. Fabric B for sashing and border
Assorted scraps for the flowers
1 yd. for backing
½ yd. for binding
37" x 37" square of batting

Cutting

Use the templates on page 62 and on pullout pattern sheet.

▶ From Fabric A, cut:
  1 square, 8½" x 8½", for Tulip Reel background
  4 rectangles, each 7½" x 16½", for Suessflower, Sunflowers, Coneflowers, and Pomegranates backgrounds
▶ From Fabric B, cut:
  4 strips, each 1½" x 16½", for sashing
  2 strips, each 5½" x 24½", for border
  2 strips, each 5½" x 34½", for border
▶ From freezer paper, make the following appliqué templates. See page 9. Use either Smoothstitch Method I or Method II. See pages 26–28.

Method I

Suessflower
  1 each, using Templates #2, #3, #4, #5, and #5r
Coneflowers
  4 Template #2
Tulip Reel
  1 Template #3
Pomegranates
  2 each, using Templates #1, #2, #3, and #3r
Sunflowers
  1 each, using Templates #2 and #4

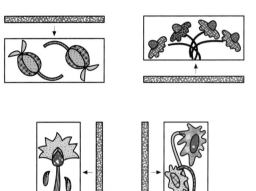

Method II

Suessflower

1 Template #1

Coneflowers

4 Template #1

Tulip Reel

4 each, using Templates #1 and #2

Sunflowers

1 each, #1 and #3

▶ From fabric scraps, cut the same number of appliqué pieces as instructed for the templates. Refer to the color photograph for color placement.

▶ Bias Stems

For Coneflowers, cut 4 strips, each 1" x 8".

For Pomegranates, cut 2 strips, each 1½" x 6".

For Sunflowers, cut 1 strip, 1½" x 12", and 1 strip, 1½" x 15".

Appliquéing and Quilt Top Assembly

1. Prepare the appliqué pieces, using the method of your choice, or follow the recommendations given on the patterns.

2. Mark placement lines on each background block. See page 28. For the Tulip Reel block, trace the design onto the background fabric in one quadrant, then rotate the background fabric and trace the design in the next quadrant. Repeat until the design is complete in all 4 quadrants.

3. Make bias stems for the Coneflowers, using the Celtic method on page 21. Make stems for the Pomegranates and Sunflowers, using the tube-turning stem method on page 30.

4. Sew the bias stems to the background blocks, before the appliqués, following the directions that begin on page 29. Place a sheet of paper or stabilizer under the stems when appliquéing to prevent puckering. Carefully remove the paper after all stems are completed.

5. Sew the appliqués in place, in numerical order.

6. Remove all freezer paper. Press the finished blocks from the wrong side.

7. Stitch a sashing strip to each of the rectangles as shown.

8. Stitch the Tulip Reel block to the Pomegranates block, leaving 2" unstitched.

Leave 2" unstitched.

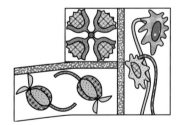

9. Sew the Sunflowers block to the right side of the resulting unit.

10. Add the Coneflowers block.

11. Add the Suess-flower block.

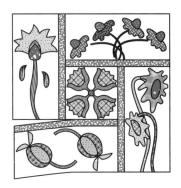

12. Finish stitching the Pomegranates block to the rest of the quilt top.

13. Sew the top and bottom border strips in place. Finally, add the side borders.

Quilt Finishing

1. Layer the quilt top with batting and backing; baste.

2. Quilt as desired and bind the edges.

Cockscomb

Finished Quilt Size: 50" x 50"
Finished Block Size: 17" x 17"
Color photo on page 32

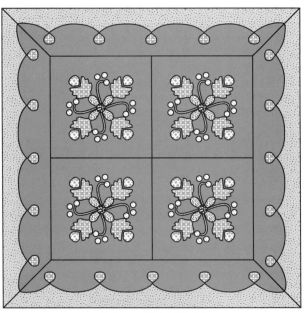

Materials: 44"-wide fabric

2½ yds. Fabric A for background
1½ yds. Fabric B for outer border and stems
⅓ yd. Fabric C (Template #1)
⅜ yd. Fabric D (Templates #2 and #5)
⅛ yd. Fabric E (Template #3)
⅛ yd. Fabric F (Template #4)
⅛ yd. Fabric G (Template #5)
3⅛ yds. for backing
½ yd. for binding
53" x 53" square of batting

Cutting

Use the templates on page 63 and on pullout pattern sheet.

▶ From freezer paper, make the following appliqué templates. See page 9. Use the Smoothstitch method of your choice as shown on pages 25–28; however, use Method II for Template #2.
　48 Template #1
　16 each, using Templates #2 and #3
　4 Template #4
　36 Template #5
　4 Template #6 (Border)

▶ From Fabric A (background), cut:
　4 squares, each 17½" x 17½"
　4 strips, each 6½" x 47¼", for inner border

▶ From Fabric B (outer border), cut:
　4 strips, each 5" x 54" (extra length allowed for trimming later)
　4 bias strips, each 1¼" x 27"

▶ From Fabric C, cut 48 Template #1

▶ From Fabric D, cut:
　16 Template #2
　20 Template #5

▶ From Fabric E, cut 16 Template #3

▶ From Fabric F, cut 4 Template #4

▶ From Fabric G, cut 16 Template #5

Appliquéing and Quilt Top Assembly

1. Prepare the appliqué pieces, using the method of your choice. See pages 25–28.

2. Make stems from the Fabric B bias strips. When completed, they will be ⅜" wide. Cut 16 stems, each 6½" long.

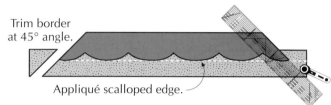

3. Mark placement lines on each background block. See page 28.

4. Sew the stems to the background blocks before the appliqués, following the directions that begin on page 29. Place a sheet of paper or stabilizer under the stems while appliquéing to prevent puckering. Carefully remove the paper.

5. Sew the appliqués in place, in numerical order.

6. Remove all freezer paper. Press the finished blocks from the wrong side.

7. Cut both ends of each inner border strip at a 45° angle as shown.

8. Position the freezer-paper pieces cut from Template #6, *shiny side up*, on top of the *wrong side* of the border strips cut from Fabric A. Match the top and side edges of the fabric and freezer paper. (The top and side seam allowances are included in the freezer-paper pattern.)

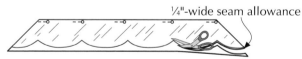

Freezer paper (shiny side up)

Fabric A (wrong side up)

Pin in place. Cut the scalloped edge from the fabric, adding a ¼"-wide seam allowance.

¼"-wide seam allowance

Fold the scalloped-edge seam allowance over onto the freezer-paper pattern and press, clipping corners as in appliqué preparation.

9. On each of the 4 Fabric B outer border strips, mark a line with a chalk wheel, 1¾" from one long edge as shown.

1¾" ↕

Chalk line

Center the inner border over the outside border, right sides up, matching the 4 inner scallops to the chalk line.

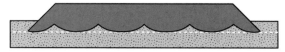

10. Fuse (dry iron, WOOL setting) the inner border to the outer border. Appliqué the scalloped edge. Trim the outer border at a 45° angle to match the inner border.

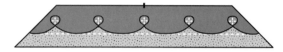

Trim border at 45° angle.

Appliqué scalloped edge.

11. Remove all freezer paper.

12. Sew the appliqués in place at the inside points of the scallops. Mark the center of the inside edge of each border strip.

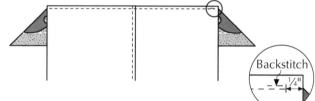

13. Using ¼"-wide seam allowances, sew the 4 blocks together.

14. Match the center marks on the border with the seams of the pieced blocks, beginning and ending the stitching ¼" from the corners. Backstitch at each end.

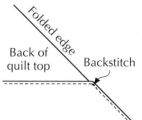

Backstitch

15. Fold the quilt top in half diagonally, right sides together. Match the scallop in the corner of the border. Stitch the corner edges together and backstitch as shown.

Folded edge
Back of quilt top
Backstitch

Quilt Finishing

Quilting designs are on the pullout pattern sheet.

1. Mark the quilting design for the corners onto the quilt top. Align the center line of the design with the seam line.

Mark the quilting design between the corners and between the blocks, first marking the center of each side, then extending the design by adding more "feathers." Do the same between the blocks.

Mark the quilting design for the corners, swags, and area between the feathers and swags.

2. Layer the quilt top with batting and backing; baste.

3. Quilt as desired and bind the edges.

A Year of Friendship

Finished Quilt Size: 22½" x 27½"
Finished Block Size: 4" x 4"
Color photo on page 31

Mimi's Friday-morning quilt group, The Catonsville Quilt and Tea Society, had a delightful quilt-block exchange last year. Each month, a member designed a small block, and each mem-

ber stitched two blocks during the first meeting of the month. They each kept one block, and a lucky member went home with the others! That lucky member designed the block for the following month. They all now have "A Year of Friendship" quilt *and* a special quilt made from their "lucky" blocks.

Members tried to keep designs simple and easy, using fusible techniques. They all love hand stitching so they used a quick "primitive" stitch to attach the appliqués.

Directions for the "Year of Friendship" quilt follow, but for added inspiration, see the photo of the "Button Baskets" quilt, made with Mimi's lucky blocks, on page 31.

Materials: 44"-wide fabric

Assorted fabrics for backgrounds
Assorted fabrics for appliqués
½ yd. solid fabric for sashing and inner border
1 yd. plaid fabric for outer border and bias binding
¾ yd. for backing
26" x 32" piece of batting
Embroidery floss to match or embellish the appliqués

Cutting

Use the templates on the pullout pattern sheet.

◗ From the assorted background fabrics, cut 12 squares, each 4½" x 4½".

◗ From the solid, cut:
17 strips, each 1½" x 4½", for sashing strips
2 strips, each 1½" x 19½", for inner top and bottom borders
2 strips, each 1½" x 16½", for inner side borders
8 squares, each 2" x 2", for pieced outer border corner squares

◗ From the plaid, cut:
2 strips, each 3½" x 16½", for side borders
2 strips, each 3½" x 21½", for top and bottom borders
8 squares, each 2" x 2", for pieced outer border corner squares
6 squares, each 1½" x 1½", for sashing squares
2"-wide bias strips, measuring a total of 110" for binding

◗ From the backing fabric, cut a 26" x 32" rectangle.

◗ From the assorted appliqué fabrics, cut appliqué pieces according to the following directions.

Appliquéing and Quilt Top Assembly

1. Trace each of the appliqué designs onto the paper side of Wonder-Under or a similar fusible product. Cut around each shape, leaving at least ¼" around the edges. The pattern shapes are printed in reverse so that they will be correct when applied to the background blocks.

2. Fuse each Wonder-Under shape to the appropriate appliqué fabric, following the manufacturer's directions. Cut out each fabric shape on the traced lines.

3. Center the appliqués in the background blocks and fuse them in place.

4. Stitch around each shape, using the buttonhole or "primitive" stitch. See page 38.

5. Following the piecing plan, sew the appliquéd blocks, sashing strips, and sashing squares together, using ¼"-wide seam allowances. Press the seams in opposite directions from row to row.

6. Sew the inner borders to the top and bottom and then to the sides of the quilt top. Press seams toward the border.

7. Sew the outer borders to the sides of the quilt top. Sew the corner squares together into four-patch units, then sew them to each end of the top and bottom outer border strips. Finally, add the top and bottom borders.

Quilt Finishing

1. Layer the quilt top with batting and backing; baste.

2. Quilt around each square, on either side of the inner border, and down the middle of the outer border.

3. Bind the edges with the plaid bias strips.

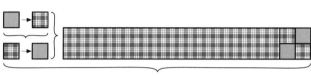

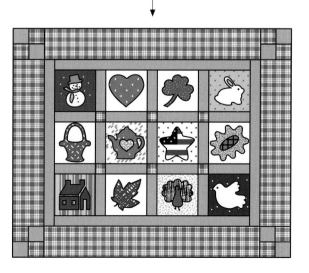

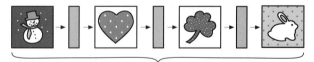

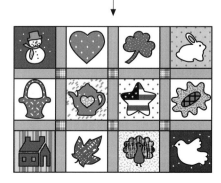

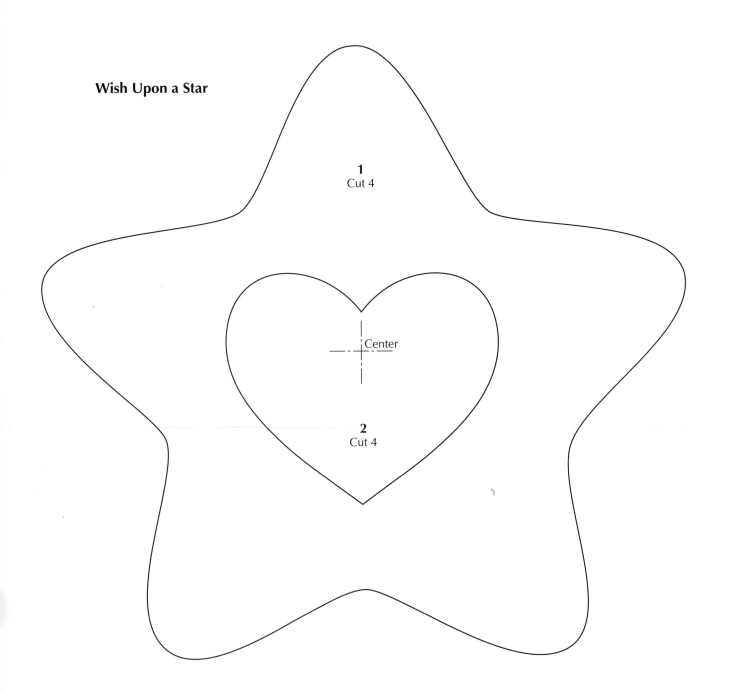

Wish Upon a Star

1
Cut 4

Center

2
Cut 4

Welcome to Baltimore
Block A

*Three-dimensional bud
(See page 22.)

Welcome to Baltimore
Block B

*Three-dimensional bud
(See page 22.)

Welcome to Baltimore
Block C

17

19

18

6

7

20

4

5

8

9*

10

13

14

Center

15

3

11

16

12

2

1

*Three-dimensional bud
(See page 22.)

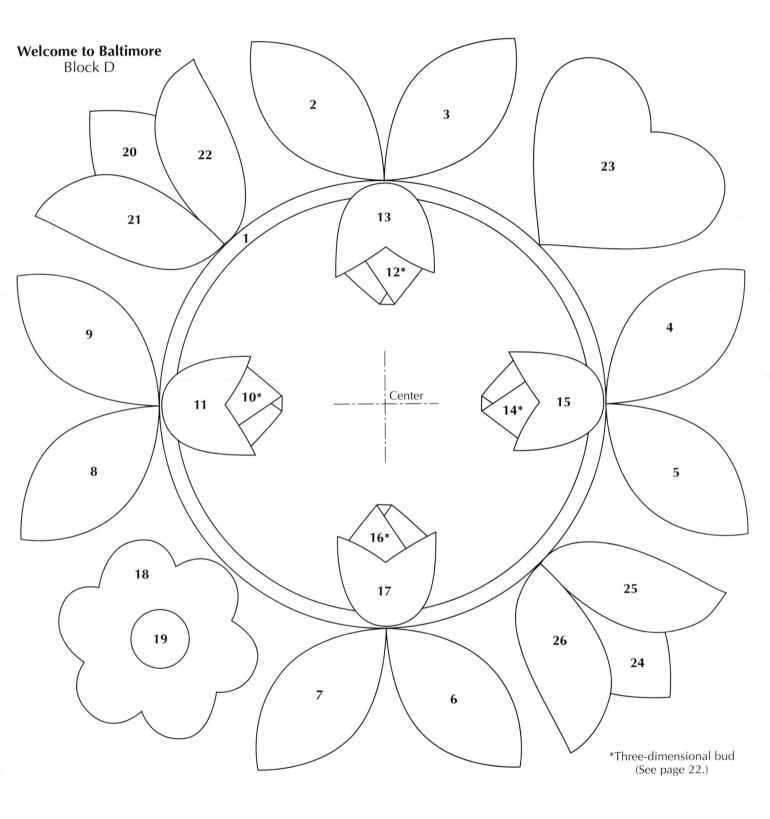

Welcome to Baltimore
Block D

1
2
3
23
20
22
21
13
12*
9
11
10*
Center
14*
15
4
8
5
16*
17
18
19
25
26
24
7
6

*Three-dimensional bud
(See page 22.)

Welcome to Baltimore
Outer Border Design

Note: See page 45 for directions for tracing outer border designs.

Make 16 swag appliqués and 12 heart appliqués.

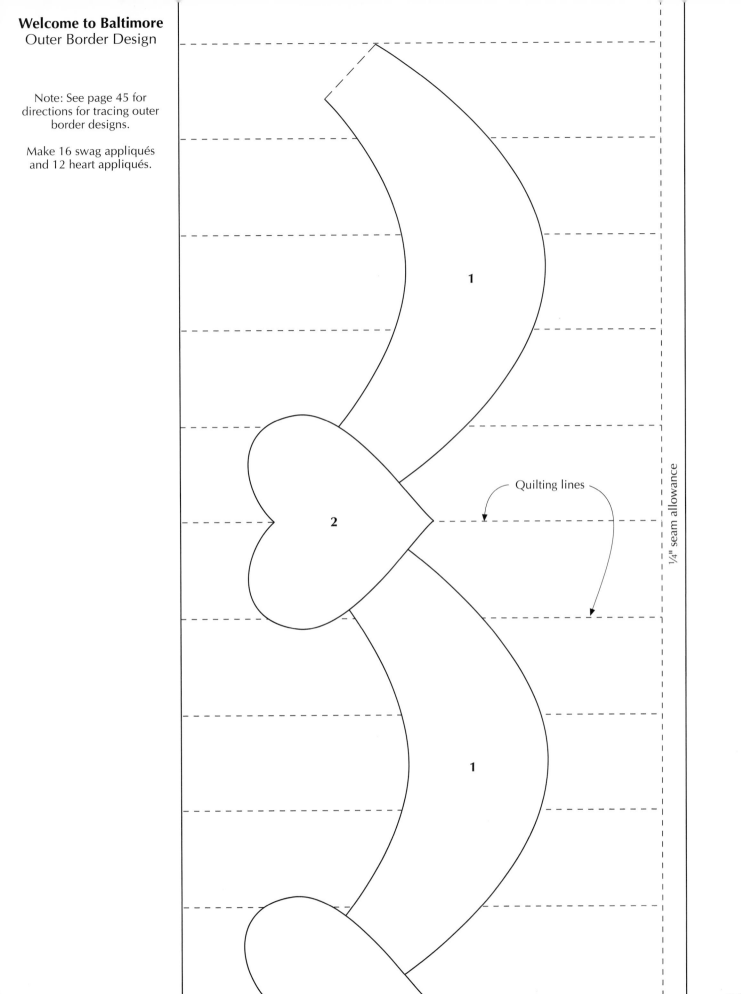

1

2

Quilting lines

1

¼" seam allowance

59

Welcome to Baltimore
Corner Design
for Outer Border

¼" seam allowance

Quilting lines

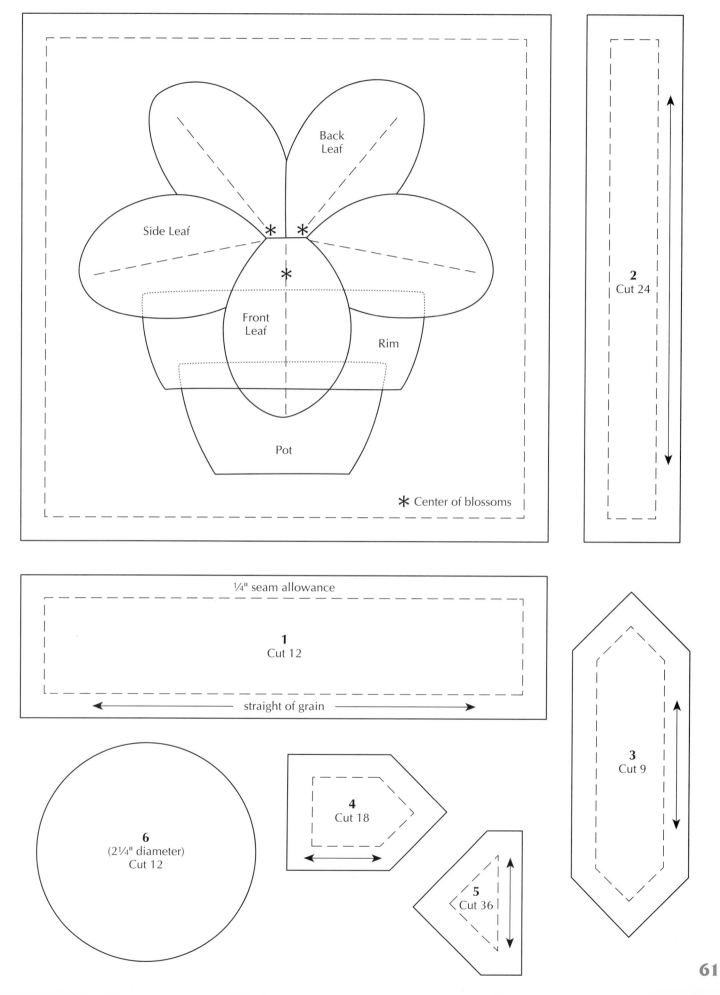

Back
Leaf

Side Leaf

Front
Leaf

Rim

Pot

* Center of blossoms

2
Cut 24

¼" seam allowance

1
Cut 12

straight of grain

6
(2¼" diameter)
Cut 12

4
Cut 18

5
Cut 36

3
Cut 9

Folk Flowers
Tulip Reel

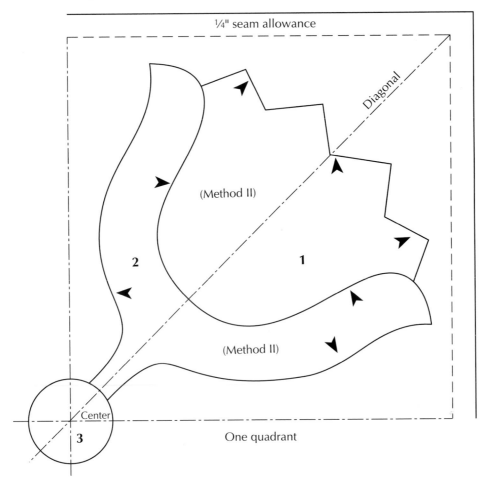

¼" seam allowance

Diagonal

(Method II)

2

1

(Method II)

Center

3

One quadrant

Complete block

Note: See page 49 for
directions for tracing the design
onto the background fabric.

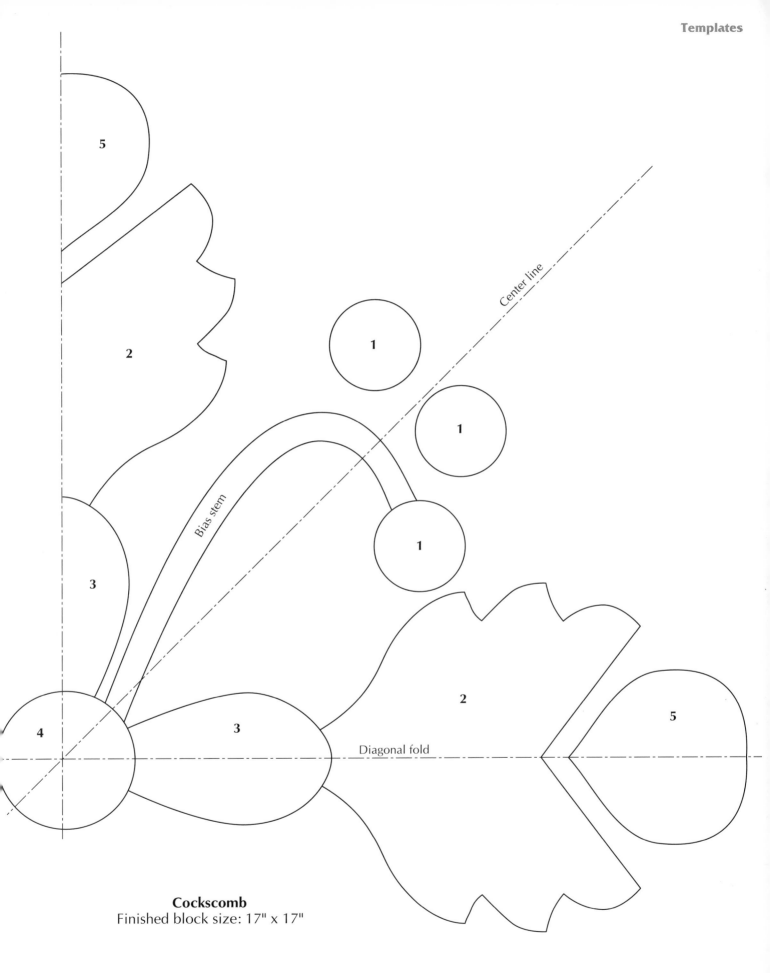

Cockscomb
Finished block size: 17" x 17"

That Patchwork Place Publications and Products

4", 6", 8", & metric Bias Square® • BiRangle™ • Ruby Beholder™ • Pineapple Rule • ScrapMaster • Rotary Rule™ • Rotary Mate™
Shortcuts to America's Best-Loved Quilts (video)

Many titles are available at your local quilt shop. For more information, send $2 for a color catalog to
That Patchwork Place, Inc., PO Box 118, Bothell WA 98041-0118 USA.

☎ Call 1-800-426-3126 for the name and location of the quilt shop nearest you.